W9-BMG-869

Tales of an African Vet

Tales of an African Vet

Dr. Roy Aronson

LYONS PRESS

Guilford, Connecticut

An imprint of Globe Pequot Press

Lyons Press is an imprint of Globe Pequot Press.

Text designer: Sheryl P. Kober
Layout: Melissa Evarts
Project editor: John Burbidge

Library of Congress Cataloging-in-Publication Data is available on file.

ISBN 978-1-59921-942-4

Printed in the United States of America

10 9 8 7 6 5 4 3 2 1

Let a person walk alone with few wishes, committing no wrong, like an elephant in the forest.

—*Gautama Buddha*

The greatness of a nation and its moral progress can be judged by the way its animals are treated.

—*Mahatma Gandhi*

Contents

Introduction

I WAS CROUCHED IN A SMALL CLEARING IN THE DENSE AFRICAN BUSH with the trackers about 10 meters (11 yards) ahead of me when all hell broke loose. The trackers had unexpectedly come across not one but three lionesses, and they had cubs. Contrary to what many people think, the first instinct of a wild animal is to run from humans. However, a lioness with cubs will stand her ground and not hesitate to attack if she feels threatened. The females facing us felt very threatened indeed. Their snarls and growls reverberated in my chest, and to put it mildly, I was terrified. The prospect of being mauled to death loomed large. Once again it crossed my mind that I should be sitting on the patio at my home in Cape Town, sipping a drink, and gazing at the calm sea. How did I wind up in the bush facing death?

My name is Roy Aronson. I am a South African veterinarian. I graduated from veterinary school in 1984 and have been in private practice ever since. In that time I have had many exciting and sometimes treacherous experiences.

I have tracked lions and cheetahs, anesthetized rhinos, collared elephants, and nearly lost a foot to a hungry crocodile. I've shot a bull running amok, come face-to-face with an angry hybrid wolf, been spat at by a cobra, and attacked by a puff adder. I have seen the devastating effects of poaching, and I've had to make some tough decisions about the fate of an animal's life time and time again.

When I think back, I realize that there were pivotal moments when my life intersected with that of an animal's, and I was forever changed. These moments have shaped my life. The animals I've helped are indelibly etched on my consciousness. The vets that I have had the privilege of working with have become personal friends. I am immeasurably richer for having met them.

In the following pages, I will introduce you to many "characters" who populate my story. You will meet the Huchzermeyers, both father and son, who are vets; Peter Rogers, a dedicated wildlife vet and one of the great ones; and Professor Dave Meltzer, a world-renowned expert on cheetah breeding. You will also meet Jabu the elephant, Munwane the rhino, Savannah the cheetah, and Mehlwane the lioness—some of the many animals I have had the amazing privilege of helping.

Many of the stories in this book came from experiences I had while filming episodes for a proposed TV show about being an African vet. Although the TV series has yet to make the screen, the lessons I learned from these people, animals, and experiences have made me a better person and a better vet. I hope that when you read these stories, some of the wisdom that has rubbed off on me will rub off on you too. There's a saying that goes like this: "Measure the risk and the reward; make sure the reward is worth the risk."

I have taken risks when working with wild and potentially dangerous animals, but the reward has been a life filled with treasured memories. Sometimes the risks my colleagues and I take can have effects so far reaching that not even in our wildest dreams could we have foretold the reward. How lucky we are to work in a profession that offers so much joy. I hope you will enjoy these stories as much as I've enjoyed being a part of them.

CHAPTER 1

Fate Almost Sealed

WHEN WE'RE YOUNG, ENTHUSIASTIC, AND PASSIONATE, SOMETIMES WE do crazy things. I have always been a determined person, and once I get the bit between my teeth, I don't like to give up. A few years before I entered veterinary school, I was serving in the South African navy. I was just twenty years old and a bit reckless then, attempting to do things that an older and wiser person may not have. I was fairly happy at the thought of how my future looked just then. My actions, however, set me on a path that I would otherwise not have trod.

I graduated from the University of Cape Town in 1975 with my first degree, a bachelor of science with majors in microbiology and biochemistry, and successfully applied to join the navy. I was based in Simon's Town, a picturesque fishing village on the stormy False Bay coast in the Western Cape about 20 miles from Cape Town itself. I was assigned to a laboratory that did quality control work in the engineering field. I was given various tasks to do, but I was also allowed to choose one or two special interest projects to keep me occupied if I had any spare time. I chose to do some investigations into antifouling paints that are used to coat ships to prevent barnacles from attaching to the hulls. If not for them, literally tons of barnacles would add massive drag to the ships. This would, of course, slow them down and dramatically increase fuel consumption. Not a good idea for a naval warship.

My project involved coating small pieces of steel with the various antifouling paints available, hanging these pieces of steel at various depths from a raft moored in the bay at Simon's Town, then measuring the number of barnacles that attached themselves. In this way I was able to assess the effectiveness of the paints and compare them so that the navy could choose the best one. I am sometimes pedantic, and the attention to detail needed in this sort of work has a certain charm to me, while it might appear tedious to others.

I was given the use of a small rowboat to access a raft moored on one side of the harbor, out of the way of passing vessels. My raft was moored next to a number of floating pontoons where seals would sun themselves. I diligently set up my experiment and hung numerous plates from ropes going down into the blue depths of the Simon's Town harbor. My experiment was designed to run for a year, through all four seasons.

I spent many happy hours rowing out to my little raft in the harbor and measuring the number of barnacles that had attached themselves to my plates that were coated with a substance designed to prevent just that. It never ceased to fascinate me how those clean, painted plates attracted and accumulated life in abundance. First the plate became slightly roughened as microscopic sea creatures attached themselves to it. Then over a period of a few days, the rough patches started to take the form of miniature barnacles that you could see with the naked eye. These grew until eventually after nearly a year they had become sea creatures coated in a hard shell. During the summer months, I'd row out with my shirt off, and when it was really hot, I'd dive into the water in my shorts and spend some time in the sun drying off before I rowed back to the shore and my lab. Clearly, this was a busy time for me. I was hard at work and having a good time. In the winter, though, it was a lot less fun. False Bay has one of the largest populations of great white sharks in the world. I kept an eye out for cruising toothy monsters that could easily reach 6 meters (20 feet) in length.

Toward the end of the first summer, I noticed that a young female seal had beached herself on a nearby pontoon. She had a distinctive marking, almost like a dark shadow around her neck. In passing, I wondered if there was a species known as a collared seal. I knew there were collared birds and lesser collared birds; perhaps there was a collared seal as well. I did not pay too much attention to her but made a mental note to be cautious because, although these sleek and engaging creatures look friendly, they can in fact be aggressive if they feel threatened and can inflict a very nasty bite if you get too close to them. I decided not to swim if she was in the vicinity.

It was three days later when I next went out to my raft. I noticed that the same young female seal was still on the pontoon. She seemed to me to be thinner than before, and the dark shadow around her neck had now taken on a reddish tinge, almost like dye running in a garment. Something was not right. It seemed strange that she was still there in the same position. The discoloration around her neck now looked sinister to me, and I decided to row back to the lab to fetch a pair of binoculars so that I could get a better look.

I arrived back at the raft about a half hour later and used the binoculars to observe the seal. To my horror, the so-called shadow around her neck was actually fishing nylon that had tangled and formed a noose that was now extremely tight and cutting into her flesh. The reddish tinge that I'd seen was blood seeping from the wound caused by the ever-tightening noose. What was I to do? I only knew that I had to help. I got back into my boat and rowed a bit closer to the pontoon where she was sitting. She must have felt very threatened because she started to bark and vocalize fiercely. Her distress and anger were obvious. Well, with the cacophony of sound coming from a mouth filled with large yellow fangs bigger than those of a German shepherd's, and a body actually twice the size of a German shepherd, weighing about 60 to 70 kilograms (132 to 154 pounds), I too felt threatened. As the gap between my boat and the pontoon closed, she panicked and dived into the sea. Clearly, this approach was not going to work.

I now had a problem that I very much wanted to solve. I turned to the Fishing Industries Research Institute, a semi-state-run research organization where marine biologists specializing in all manner of sea creatures worked. A member of their staff was an expert in marine mammals. I was convinced that this was a fairly common problem, and I hoped that he would be able to help me solve it. I called him, and our discussion did bear some fruit, although in an oblique way. He informed me that there were no fast-acting drugs available to inject or dart seals. Once darted, the seal would take fright, swim away, and be long gone by the time the drugs took effect. Now deep underwater and impossible to find, the seal would slip into dreamland and drown. To my surprise, he explained that there was no protocol for this problem. Each time something like this came their way, it was dealt with on an ad hoc basis. He felt that the only way to save the seal was to actually capture her in a net. Once netted, she could be safely immobilized with a sedative without the risk of drowning. Alternatively, if the seal was small enough, he recommended muzzling her and then wrestling her into a position where the noose could be removed. Given the size of her teeth, the sedative option seemed more attractive to me at the time.

Armed with this plan, I contacted a local vet and explained the problem to him. He very kindly volunteered his help. This was progress indeed. I obtained a large net from the navy storage warehouse, and I made a long pole with a big loop of stiff wire at the end. I sewed the net into a bag large enough to capture the seal and attached it to the wire loop. Once all my equipment was ready, I contacted the vet. He drove out to the dockyard, where we boarded the rowboat and confidently set off to capture our seal. How naive we were!

Before we could get close enough to net the seal, she sounded her alarm by barking frantically, after which she dived into the water and swam off without a backward glance. The vet kindly offered to wait for a while, so we bobbed up and down in the water just off the pontoon for a half hour. After this time, it was clear that the seal was not coming back, so we had to abandon the plan and row back to shore. I was now on my own, and while pondering the problem, I looked through the binoculars to try to get a view of the pontoon. Lo and behold, our seal was back on the pontoon sunning herself. Once we had departed, she must have felt safe enough to return.

The next few weeks were a stalemate. Every time I approached the pontoon, she would dive into the water and swim away, not letting me come even remotely close to her. The only small consolation was that she returned to the pontoon time and time again. She must have felt safe there, because out in the open ocean, debilitated as she was, she was a sitting target for any number of predators. False Bay has a large population of seals and a large population of great whites that prey on them, and this injured seal would make a quick and easy snack for a cruising great white. It was amazing that she had survived thus far.

She was now even thinner. I noticed that her forays into the sea were getting shorter, and the time she spent lying on the pontoon was getting longer. I wondered if she was eating. Seals are hunters and need to be fully agile and healthy in order to hunt successfully. This seal was getting weaker and thinner, and I was sure that her success as a hunter was being compromised.

I decided to try to feed her and went to a local shop in Simon's Town to buy some fresh fish. I got the fishmonger to cut the fish into what I considered to be bite-size snacks for a seal, then rowed out as close to the pontoon as I could get without startling her. By now she was getting used to me, and I was learning about her boundaries. I knew how close I could get before she would jump off and swim away, and it seemed to me that I was able to get closer and closer each day. I wondered if this was because she was getting used to me or because she was simply getting weaker by the day.

I rowed up to a distance that did not frighten her and threw a piece of fish onto the pontoon about a meter (3 feet) away from her. To my disappointment, she did not make any effort to try to eat it. I threw another piece, closer to her this time, but still she ignored it. I decided to row a bit closer and throw fish into the water, hoping that she would jump off the pontoon and feed from the fish pieces in the water. But this did not work either. I now realized that despite my best efforts to help her, there was a real possibility that the seal would die. I was compelled to help, though.

She had crossed my path and, to my mind, had become my responsibility.

I sat in the rowboat, bobbing up and down a few meters from the pontoon, feeling frustrated and dejected. Was this beautiful animal going to die? Was there no way to get close enough to her to sever the nylon that had embedded itself around her neck?

I continued to ask people for help, and each time someone would come up with a new suggestion as to how to capture her or immobilize her. But no matter who tried or what was tried, we got the same result. When she felt threatened by human proximity, she would jump into the safety of the water and swim off. She returned only when we had retreated a safe distance.

The hours became days and the days weeks, and she became weaker and weaker. After a month of trying everything I could think of, she was so weak that I was finally able to sit on the pontoon a meter away from her without her jumping into the sea to escape. But it was just not close enough to cut the nylon. She was dying, and I felt totally useless.

At this point, fate took an unexpected and very welcome hand in the matter. The expert I had called at the Fishing Industries Research Unit called me to ask how things were going. I told him my sorry tale and said that unless something drastic happened, she would die within a few days. He offered to come out the next day to see what we could do together. I thanked him gratefully for what I considered to be an eleventh-hour reprieve. The next morning, I went to work with considerably raised spirits. My contact arrived with a bag filled with equipment, including a special throw net that had a leather hood. He told me that since the seal was so weak, we could try to throw the hooded net over her, immobilize her mouth, and prevent her from diving into the sea. He also had a pair of scissors with long handles and a pair of heavy leather gloves. Equipped with this bag of tricks and newfound hope, we rowed out to the pontoon. The seal was lying there and was a depressing sight. Her eyes were dull, and her fur lacked luster. I was sure that she was near death. We were able to get onto the pontoon without her moving away, and I think that at this point she was just too weak to offer any meaningful resistance. I doubt that she would have been able to swim had she had the strength to jump off the pontoon.

My friend donned the heavy leather gloves and with a casual but experienced flick of his wrist threw the net over the recumbent seal. He quickly grabbed the ends of the net in case she jumped off the pontoon and maneuvered the hood over her head. He then managed to sit astride the seal, something I have no doubt he would have been unable to do if she had been healthy and up to full strength. In the meantime, I had grabbed the long-handled scissors and quickly went to work cutting through the heavy line around her neck. At long last the noose of death was off, but I wondered if it was too late. Now all we could do was inject her with antibiotics and an anti-inflammatory and hope for the best.

Nature is a wonderful thing. Given the opportunity, once the underlying cause has been removed, most animals will heal themselves, even in such an advanced state of debility as the seal was in.

I watched her with wonder as the next two weeks passed. The first thing I noticed was that even by the next day, a scant twenty-four hours later, she started swimming a bit more and lying on the pontoon a bit less. Within another day or two, her coat started to regain some of its beautiful luster. After a week she was swimming vigorously and spending less and less time on the pontoon. I had no doubt that she was able to hunt now because she actually started putting on weight at an amazing rate. From day to day I could see the difference. The cut around her neck was healing, and the seeping had stopped. The dark ring of fur was still there, and I wondered if the fur might not be permanently stained. Blood is a strong attractant to sharks, and her instincts must have made her aware of this, because she never really strayed outside the harbor precincts during her recovery.

The last time I saw her on the pontoon was two weeks after we had removed the noose. She was once again sleek and, dare I say, almost fat. Her wound had healed completely, and there was no blood seepage, but the dark ring, probably a lifelong memento from the cruel necklace she had worn for at least five or six weeks, was still there. When I came too close, she barked loudly and dived into the water.

And then one day she just was not there anymore. I guessed that she had recovered fully and was now able to resume her life as a seal in the open ocean.

A few months later while I was working on my raft and measuring barnacle growth, I looked up and caught a glimpse of a sleek and fat seal, about the same size as the one I had helped. The seal jumped onto the pontoon for a few seconds and then dived off and swam away, but not before I noticed a black ring of fur around its neck. The experience had left its own indelible mark on me as well, and I decided soon after that I would apply to veterinary school.

CHAPTER 2

A Ride on the wild Side

I WAS HUNTING FOR EQUIPMENT FOR MY FLEDGLING FARRIER CAREER AT a marvelous shop in Pretoria (the legislative capital of South Africa) called Lion Bridge. I was in my first year of veterinary science and had five and a half years of hard work and hopefully harder play ahead of me. Lion Bridge sold a great selection of farrier tools, horseshoes, and various pieces of hardware associated with farriery. Farrier science is the art of placing steel shoes on horses' feet using, believe it or not, a hammer and nails, and I had acquired this skill because I once owned a horse with a problem hoof that I learned to care for myself. I was trying to purchase shoeing nails and was discussing the various options with the salesman. Our conversation must have been overheard, because a rugged-looking man stepped into our field of vision and asked me if I was a farrier. Well, I was not just a farrier, I was also a veterinary student in my first year of studying to become a vet. I was twenty-five at the time of this fortuitous meeting. What lofty heights I had attained!

He took my hand in a viselike grip and said by way of introduction, "My name is Clive Steyn, and I have a private game reserve in the Tuli Block in Botswana." He explained that he had twelve horses on the game reserve, and as a special service he took people for horseback safaris. The horses needed hoof care, and there were no farriers in the area. If I was prepared to come to his farm, he would host me and my wife, Kathy (also a vet student), as his guests. In return I would care for his horses' feet and deworm them and do many of the routine things that needed to be done. What an opportunity! I thought. I had never been to Botswana and instantly accepted his offer. We swapped names, addresses, and telephone numbers and agreed to be in touch with each other within the week to arrange the trip.

There were no other enterprises like his that I had heard of. Offering horseback safaris in the wild African bush thirty years ago was visionary, but then Clive was at least twenty or more years ahead of his time.

I finished my purchases and rushed home to share this great news with Kathy. We got out a map and looked at the Tuli Block, a long, thin stretch of land along the southeastern border of Botswana. We noted how far Clive's farm was from where we lived and guessed that it would take us about four hours to drive from our house in Pretoria north to his farm, located near a small town called Sherwood Ranch on the Limpopo River. Even the names of these places sounded romantic. The line from Rudyard Kipling's story "The Elephant's Child" played over in my head: "On the banks of the great gray greasy Limpopo River." I remember this well from my childhood.

To my surprise, Clive must have been even keener than we were, because he called me that same evening to once again invite us to come to his farm. We would drive there on the last weekend of the month, two weeks away. I guess his horses' feet must have been in serious need of attention for him to be so eager. This all happened before the invention of satellite navigation, so he gave us detailed directions over the phone, and we agreed to leave our home around noon to get there by early evening.

Clive briefed me about the horses and what needed doing, and over the next two weeks I made my preparations. I made sure that my tools were sharp and well oiled, and I laid in a stock of deworming pastes. I had just obtained a large cowhide and had made a great farrier apron out of it. (Little did I know that this item of apparel would create quite a stir at the Botswana border.)

When it was time to leave, our car was heavily laden with luggage, equipment, and, oddly enough, lots of fresh produce like tomatoes and lettuce. Clive told us that they were far from a store that sold fresh produce, and we must bring a good supply for the weekend.

The journey to the Botswana border was uneventful. The last town on the South African side was Pietersburg. It was a short drive from there to the Limpopo River. On the South African side of the river, we went through the border post and customs office without a problem. When we crossed the Limpopo into Botswana and went to the equivalent office, however, we were approached by a large uniformed official bristling with hostility.

At the time, apartheid in South Africa was alive and well, and we were white and therefore perceived as the bad guys from the south. The official barked at us and gave us forms to fill out and asked us if we had anything to declare. He specifically asked us if we had "hidesanskins." I looked at him and tried to fathom what on earth he was talking about. What was "hidesanskins"? After filling out his forms, we were told he wanted to search our car. We had nothing to hide, so we willingly opened up the car. He proceeded to unpack our carefully packed belongings and started to rummage through my tools and equipment. All we could do was look on helplessly. Suddenly he found my farrier apron, and gleefully he almost started dancing with the apron in his hand, chanting "hidesanskins." I suddenly realized that he had asked us if we had hides or skins with us. Botswana had foot and mouth disease, and the importing and exporting of cattle products of any form was strictly controlled. At last I was making some sense of all of this. He wanted to confiscate my beautiful and highly useful farrier apron. I started to protest loudly and asked to see the commanding officer. I must have made quite a fuss, because within a few minutes, a smart, well-spoken man came outside to see what the hullabaloo was about. He identified himself as the commanding officer of the Sherwood Ranch border post. I told him that one of his customs officials was confiscating a piece of my equipment, and I objected strongly to this. To my surprise, he was a very reasonable man and started to ask me where I had got the piece of skin. I told him that it was a properly cured hide, and I had purchased it from a reliable source. He seemed to have some knowledge of skins, because he took the apron and examined it carefully on both sides. After a tense moment he declared that the hide was properly cured and posed no threat of foot and mouth disease, and I could keep it. I was relieved because the strong leather apron was truly a great protection against injury when working with horses' hooves.

Amazingly, he expedited the entire crossing. Within a few moments we were packed, albeit not as neatly as when we set off, and on our way.

The crossing from South Africa to Botswana is sudden. You not only cross a physical barrier, namely, the Limpopo River, but you seem to cross a cultural and psychological barrier as well. The South African side has paved roads and recent-model automobiles. There is a sense of hustle and bustle. The Botswana side has dirt roads and the odd person walking along them. Even today, the sense that one is in wild Africa is more pronounced north of our borders.

After we crossed the border, cars were few and far between, and when we did see one, it was usually a truck or a dilapidated sedan. There was a sense of desolation, and it made me uneasy. I came from a country rich in resources. We were now traveling in a country far less fortunate than our own.

We had detailed instructions about how to proceed to Sherwood Ranch, about 10 kilometers (6 miles) from the border crossing. Once in the small town, we would drive another 10 kilometers to the gates of the farm, then another 10 kilometers of farm road to the actual farmhouse and lodge, on the banks of the Limpopo. By now, with the delay at the border post, it was after five, and the sun was low in the sky. That magnificent time of day, where everything seems red in the dying sun, was nearly upon us. We still had 30 kilometers of driving along dirt roads, and this would take us the better part of an hour. We hoped we would arrive at the lodge just in time for a sunset drink.

At six o'clock we drove into the parking lot outside the lodge, tired, dusty, and glad we were safe. We were approached by a young woman about our age. She introduced herself as Jane and said she was Clive's "lady friend." Now, I know that Clive was at least fifty years old, and Jane was not more than twenty-four or twenty-five, so here was another interesting facet to this already fascinating man.

She seemed to be in charge of the entire operation. She told us that Clive would not be making it that weekend, but she was there to entertain us and show us which horses would need my tender ministrations. She showed us to our thatched huts and gave us a few moments to freshen up, then we were to join her for cocktails around the fire in the *lapa,* a reed enclosure with no roof.

We wasted no time, and within ten minutes we were showered and changed and clinking ice in tall glasses filled with gin and tonic and a touch of angostura bitters. Life could be worse.

Supper was prepared by the resident chef. One of the many amazing things we were to experience that weekend was the "stove" on which dinner was prepared. It was a four-plate bush stove. This consisted of a large metal frame placed over a fire pit. The metal frame had special places where a number of round iron pots could be individually set. Alongside these spaces for pots there was a barbecue grill for cooking meat directly on the flames or coals, depending on the chef's menu. The fire was spread evenly under the metal contraption, and the heat was turned up or down by placing more or less coal under each individual spot. In this way a veritable banquet could be easily prepared with all the courses coming together at the right time. This item of equipment was truly a bush marvel—simplicity itself but elegantly efficient.

We had supplied some of the fresh produce for the salad, but the rest of the meal was supplied by our host. We ate and then ate some more, and when we were all completely satisfied, we had a nightcap and went to bed early, because by the sound of what Jane had told us that night, I was going to have a busy time the next day "paying" for our supper.

We made our way to our hut using the flashlight we had brought with us. At the entrance there was a small front porch with two comfortable chairs. Kathy and I sank into these chairs, and we switched the flashlight off and sat mesmerized by the sounds of Africa and the stupendous night sky. Without the torch and without any man-made light to illuminate the sky, thousands of stars not usually visible sprang out to greet us. Reluctantly, after a few minutes we stood up and walked tiredly to our beds. Tomorrow was a big day. We had work to do and a game reserve to explore.

The next day we woke refreshed and eager to get going. It was still early, and I wanted to get immersed in my work before the day got too hot. I had told Jane about my way of doing things the previous evening, so the staff and the horses were prepared.

I am not going to go into detail about the pain and suffering associated with attending to the feet of at least a dozen horses. Suffice it to say that by the end of the morning, I had sweated buckets and absolutely earned my holiday. Kathy did her fair share as well. She was in charge of the "postop" care. Once the feet were done, she would take the horses and deworm them, check their teeth and file them if needed, and attend to the rest of their health checks and maintenance. In this way we worked as a team.

I must stress that at the time we were not qualified vets, but all the procedures that we did on these and many other horses we cared for during our student years were legal procedures that we laypeople were allowed to perform. We used only products and equipment that unqualified students were allowed to use. We were very careful to avoid using illegal or licensed products, and we never stepped on any vet's toes, not even slightly.

The special thing about Clive's operation was that he allowed his guests to ride horses throughout his game reserve. The reserve was a farm on the Tuli Block, and he owned a 5-kilometer (3-mile) stretch of river front on the Limpopo. The farm measured some 5 by 20 kilometers (3 by 12 miles), about 100 square kilometers, or about 40 square miles. This was a lot of land, and riding a horse through the veld was a fantastic way of viewing game. He had told us that there were no dangerous predators on the farm, but this was wild Africa, and one never did know for sure. Botswana is home to the African "Big Five"—lions, elephants, rhinos, buffalo, and leopards—as well as any other wild African animal you can think of and a whole lot you probably have never heard of. I think that a lot of the thrill of riding through the bush is the anticipation of seeing something completely unexpected, like a lion that should not have been there. The other amazing thing about riding horses in the bush is that the wild animals accept the horses and their riders without spooking. A man on horseback seems not to be recognized as a man but possibly as just another animal in the bush. We had heard all this, and now we were going to experience it firsthand.

The afternoon went by quickly, and at about quarter to four, we changed into comfortable riding gear and riding boots and went over to the stable complex, which consisted of a tack room and some fenced paddocks and a lapa-like structure with a large reed roof affording the horses shelter should the weather turn bad. The tack on hand was old but very comfortable, and we were given horses to suit our ability as riders. The horses were well schooled and appeared well looked after. We were going to be taken for a game ride by Shadrak, the chief warden on the reserve and a native of Botswana, while Jane stayed behind. We mounted our horses and, following Shadrak into the bush, started out on what was to be one of the great experiences of my life.

As the horses walked quietly off into the thick bush, the saddles creaked a little under our seats. This was a comforting sound, the sound that a well-worn leather sofa makes when you settle into it. The bridle and bit also made their own quiet tinkling sounds, and the thud of the hooves was muffled by the thick sand underfoot. The horses occasionally brushed aside small bushes and branches, and the rustling this made added to the beauty of the experience. Our talking was kept to a minimum, and all commands were given by hand. If Shadrak wanted us to go in any direction, he snapped his fingers to attract our attention, then pointed to an area in the distance. If he wanted us to see something, he used the same technique.

The sounds of Africa were magnified in the silence. The air was filled with bird and insect sounds. On horseback our heads were at least a meter and a half (about 5 feet) higher than usual, so the panorama was so much wider than on foot. The most thrilling thing of all is that when we approached game on horseback, they didn't seem to recognize us as human. To them, we must have appeared as some sort of mythical beasts, half human and half horse.

Our first encounter was with a small herd of kudu. These magnificent animals are usually shy and run at the first sight of humans. The males have long horns for fighting in pursuit of females during mating, and also for defense. The females don't have horns, and their large eyes and biggish ears give them an innocence that is enchanting. We rode steadily into the small herd and sat quietly as the horses mingled with the kudu. I have never encountered kudu from such close range. They did not even stop their browsing, but carried on munching the leaves from their favorite trees. Shadrak did not need to guide the horses; they continued to mingle with the herd for a few magical moments and then quietly moved on.

We headed south toward the Limpopo. The camp was near the riverbank, and from the lofty height of the horses' backs, we could clearly see the green riverine trees sharply defined from the rest of the dusty colored bushes. Shadrak drew our attention and quietly told us that we were going to see if there were any hippos about. Since more people are killed by hippos in Africa than by any other animal, I was quite anxious at this announcement. I was, however, not going to be the one to chicken out. With a nervous swallow, I allowed my horse to follow Shadrak's.

We threaded our way through the bush, and suddenly Shadrak's horse gave a snort and shied sideways. He was nearly unseated but managed to stay on. We all had quite a start and quickly looked around to see why the horse had spooked. Just a few feet ahead of his horse, we saw a very large snake. It was a python, and it was at least 25 centimeters (10 inches) thick. It continued to slither into the bush, and just as suddenly as it appeared, it disappeared. The markings on its body were beautiful, an intricate pattern of olive green, beige, and black, allowing it to blend exquisitely into its bushy surroundings. I wished that I had seen the whole thing, head and all. Shadrak told us that there were python nests nearby and that they did not pose a threat to a person on horseback. We resumed our march through the thin riverine tree zone toward the river and the hippos.

Abruptly the trees and bush opened up, and there before us was the mighty Limpopo. And a mighty river it was, stretching for thousands of kilometers and carrying millions of tons of fresh water as it bisected Africa along the northern border of South Africa, passing through numerous countries as it wended its way toward the sea. At the point where our adventure intersected this mighty river, it was about 200 meters wide (220 yards), and Shadrak told us that it was also many meters deep at the center. The banks were sandy, and there, in what must have been a wallow about a meter (3 feet) or so deep, we looked on a mighty gathering of hippos. These massive animals usually either lie on the sandy banks or stand on the riverbed immersed in the water. Some were on the banks slumbering, but most were in the water with just their ears, eyes, and nostrils above water so that they could hear, see, and breathe. I marveled once again at the ease of access our horses allowed us. I have approached hippos on foot, but they take fright and charge off, and sometimes they've charged me too. This time, however, they seemed as equally ambivalent of us as they were of the horses.

Shadrak bade us stay still, and we did just that. We sat quietly on our mounts and observed these hippos in their natural habitat from a distance of about 20 meters (22 yards). We watched them quietly grazing on the banks, we watched them lumber as they walked in the water, half floating and half walking. We watched a large male yawn and gasped at the extent that he could open his mouth and were intimidated by his massive ivory fangs that must have been nearly 50 centimeters (20 inches) long. We trembled when this male moved aggressively toward a smaller rival male in a display of strength that left no doubt who was in charge. Then, silently, Shadrak signaled for us to exit from this amazing place in the same direction from which we had come.

Thirty years later, I can still taste the dust in my throat and feel the tingle of excitement in my belly when I think back to this time. The sweat expended on that day has long since dried, the difficulty of attending to twelve horses in the African bush has long been forgotten, but the priceless memories of our first ride in the bush will last to our grave. We would visit Clive's wonderful reserve many times during our careers as students at the University of Pretoria. We took friends with us on numerous occasions, and each time we experienced the magic of riding in the bush. And the skills as a farrier I honed at Tuli would serve me well on various animals, including a lame rhinoceros at the Pretoria Zoo.

Chapter 3

All for a Piece of Horn

THE SO-CALLED APHRODISIAC PROPERTIES OF RHINO HORN ARE GREATLY exaggerated. I have personally had the opportunity to try some. I was once offered some in the form of a tea brewed by steeping rhino horn powder in hot water. I can vouch for the fact that this did not lead to any fireworks for me, in or out of the bedroom.

What, may you ask, was a vet doing trying rhino horn when his whole philosophy is preserving the lives of both wildlife and domestic animals? Allow me to explain. In our final year of study, we did ambulatory clinics, traveling all over greater Pretoria caring for animals. One of the places we worked at was the Pretoria Zoo, where a rhino resided. This large animal was about fourteen years old, and his horn was large, about 1 meter (3 feet) in length and a good 30 centimeters (12 inches) in diameter at its base. A rhino's "horn" is actually made up of very densely matted hair and is not technically a horn at all.

There was a large steel gate at the entrance to his enclosure, the bars of which were just wide enough apart to allow the rhino to insert his horn through them. Once this was accomplished, he would rub his horn back and forth across the bars.

We assumed that he must have had an itch at the base of his horn. He had been doing this routine for years. His itch just never seemed to get better. Every time he did this, he scraped rhino horn powder off the base of his horn. This powder was then collected by the staff of the zoo and sold to the *muti* shop (African medicine shop) for quite a large sum of money. It is a sad fact that without rigorous laws and their enforcement, rhinos would probably have been poached to extinction for the mythical and nonsensical properties attributed to their horn. There was, however, no need to kill the rhino this time for its horn; instead, the patient zoo staff collected the small amounts daily, and when the volume was large enough, it was sold. This really was a continuously renewable source of rhino horn, and the zoo authorities turned a blind eye to this enterprise led by the zoo assistants who worked with the rhino. The head veterinarian of the zoo at that time was Dr. Hymie Ebedes, and he had a small supply of rhino horn that he kept locked in a cupboard in his office. When we were students, we did some work there, and some of us were offered a small amount of rhino horn tea. I took some out of curiosity and really can vouch for its ineffectiveness.

I was in my final year of veterinary science. I was doing quite a lot of farrier work and was somewhat of a self-proclaimed expert in foot and hoof care. Besides having an itchy horn, the rhino in question was also lame and had been walking around limping on his sore foot for a few weeks now. Dr. Ebedes asked me if I was prepared to examine and treat the affected foot. Needless to say, I jumped at the opportunity. Well, maybe *jump* is the wrong word. One cannot just saunter up to a 2-ton rhino and ask it to allow you to examine its foot. That would be very foolish. As with all wild and game animals, the examination procedure takes place under general anesthesia.

Using a drug known as M99 (etorphine hydrochloride), Dr. Ebedes shot the rhino in its rump with a dart gun. We then settled down on the outside of the perimeter wall to wait for the drug to take effect. This usually took about six minutes. Another drug called ACP (acepromazine) is usually administered with M99. This too had been done by Dr. Ebedes, but it seemed as though this rhino required a bigger dose of ACP than it had received, because instead of settling quietly and going to sleep, it became agitated and suddenly started to stumble around its enclosure. We all looked on in horror as within the space of a few seconds the rhino charged toward a wall some 50 meters (55 yards) away. Now, when 2 tons of rhino collides with an immovable object such as a reinforced solid concrete wall, something has to give. Because of the small size of the enclosure and the effect of the drugs, the rhino luckily struck the wall horn first at half speed, but it was still a shock. We all stared, mouths agape, as the drama unfolded. The rhino crumpled against the wall. The noise of flesh colliding with concrete was sickening. The rhino was snorting and squealing, and there was a loud ripping sound as its entire horn was torn off. In effect, the rhino had been scalped.

For a few seconds after the impact, there was complete silence. The rhino lay utterly still next to the wall. Then out of the stillness a member of the zoo staff suddenly jumped headlong into the enclosure. He was dressed like all other housekeeping staff in blue overalls, and he was moving so fast that he was difficult to identify. This person had seen an opportunity and grabbed it with both hands, literally. He ran to the horn that lay in the dust, scooped it up, and sped like a man possessed. As soon as he had neared the wall, he threw the horn to what looked like a waiting friend. Like a relay race, this friend then ran with the horn for a short distance, until he too threw the horn to a third person. This went on for a short while, possibly under a minute. The net result was that the horn must have changed hands about ten times in that minute and was spirited out of the zoo. We learned later that it was sold for a vast sum of money to the muti shop. It must have been impossible to resist the opportunity to earn half a year's salary for just a few minutes' effort.

What we had just witnessed was so astonishing that it really bears dwelling on for a moment. It unfolded as though it had been rehearsed many times, although how it could have been anticipated no one knew. There were about ten participants in the event. Person number one who jumped in and grabbed the horn initiated it. He then ran to the perimeter wall before passing it to person number two. Then in a series of passes that would have made a national rugby team proud, the horn simply disappeared.

The vets and we students just stood and gaped in stunned amazement for that moment before shaking ourselves out of our stupor. Then we too were galvanized into action. Our action, however, was not directed at horn retrieval but rather at the safety and well-being of our charge. We jumped down into the enclosure and ran to the recumbent rhino. Was it unconscious, or was it dead from the dreadful impact?

When we surrounded the animal and allowed Dr. Ebedes to examine it, to our immense relief it was found to be sleeping with only its large horn missing to remind us of the impact. The concrete reinforced wall, on the other hand, was unscathed. In place of the horn, there was a large raw wound about 30 centimeters (12 inches) in diameter. Fortunately, it was a very superficial wound that would heal fairly easily, and eventually another horn would grow in its place.

After all the excitement, we almost forgot why we anesthetized the rhino in the first place, but once the situation returned to normal, we were able to get down to the business of treating the rhino's injured foot.

The rhino was lying on its side. The anesthetic was stable, and he was now sleeping peacefully. The anesthetic would last for about an hour or until it was reversed using a specific antidote, so we had time to do the job properly. All four limbs were protruding to the side, and we were able to examine them with relative ease. I had brought along my tools for treating hooves, and Dr. Ebedes and I started to examine all four feet. We had decided to also trim and file the nails on each toe of each foot. I set about doing this, while Dr. Ebedes continued with the examination. A rhino's foot has three toes, and each toe has a thick, strong nail. Once I had finished trimming the toes, he called me to examine the painful foot that was causing the lameness. It looked to me as though there was an abscess under the foot. There was an area about 5 centimeters (2 inches) in diameter that was discolored. I took a paring knife and started to open the area in question. I had cut only a short way before I hit a pocket of pus that gushed out under pressure from the wound. I dug a little deeper and then came across the cause of the abscess. There was a large thorn that had burrowed its way into the animal's foot and festered there, causing pain and discomfort. Dr. Ebedes theorized that the pain may have been so intense that it canceled out the sedating effect of ACP, thus causing the rhino's collision with the wall.

Once all the pus had been drained and the thorn removed, we flushed the wound out thoroughly and packed it with a special antiseptic powder. We then injected the rhino with antibiotics, and Dr. Ebedes injected the antidote called M50 50 intravenously.

The rhino woke up and stumbled to its feet. It stood a while and shook its head. Usually after the anesthetic is reversed, animals stand up and act almost as though nothing has happened. This rhino, however, stumbled around for a few days after the treatment. We were not sure if this was due to the foot having been worked on or due to the massive collision between its head and the wall, which may have caused a concussion. Within a few days, however, all was back to normal.

The rhino lived another seventeen years at the zoo. Its horn did grow back, but it never again was a meter in length. The rhino still rubbed the base of its horn between the bars once there was enough horn to scrape. I would have thought that the loss of its first horn would have cured any itch, but maybe it was just a bad habit or a nervous tic that caused him to do this. Nevertheless, the continuous source of powdered rhino horn carried on until his death in 2001.

Rhino horn, unfortunately, is still a commodity that has value in certain circles. It is believed by some to be an aphrodisiac, and because of this, rhinos to this day are still poached. The only way to stop the slaughter of these magnificent animals is to educate the "users" of rhino horn specifically and the general population at large that there are no benefits to consuming rhino horn at all. The horn is best left on the rhino, where it serves a marvelous purpose, as opposed to being consumed by people who accrue no benefit whatsoever from its consumption.

When Kathy and I finally qualified as veterinarians, we high-tailed it back to our home in Cape Town, where we decided to set up in private practice by ourselves. Normally, a new vet joins an existing practice, where he or she learns the tools of the trade and gains experience from seasoned colleagues. Not us, though; we thought we knew it all. We did, however, need an income until our fledgling private practice was able to keep us clothed and fed. I had to moonlight and take another job at the Cape Town abattoir, where many other interesting adventures occurred. The one that stands out most, however, nearly cost me my life.

CHAPTER 4

The Bull Shooter

STARING DOWN THE BARREL OF A RIFLE, FACING THE WRATH OF A charging bull, was not my idea of fun. With trembling hands and a very dry mouth, I started to squeeze the trigger, fully expecting to clamp my eyes shut with fright as the rifle went off. How on earth did I get myself into this crazy situation?

I had taken out a loan from the City of Cape Town during my final year of veterinary school. Once I qualified as a vet, I had two options with regard to repayment. I could either pay back the sum loaned as a cash payment, or I could take a job with the Cape City Council. For each year they supported me, I had to work for them for one year. I thought that this was a better option, so after qualifying, I came back to Cape Town and started working for the city. What I did not realize was that my job would entail working for the city abattoir.

An abattoir is a grim place. It is here that live, healthy animals are turned into meat and by-products. A vet's job is crucial in an abattoir. He or she makes sure that all animals slaughtered are treated humanely. This sounds like a contradiction in terms, but if you think about it, it will seem obvious. Cruelty in the handling and loading and transportation of animals is prevented by the vet. The actual slaughter process must be quick and painless. The vet must oversee the well-being and safety of the animals for the short time that they stay there. The vet also confirms that all meat coming from the abattoir is fit for human consumption. If an animal is sick at the time of slaughter, the carcass is inspected, and if the disease is transmissible to humans or in any way spoils the meat, then that animal's carcass is condemned and destroyed.

Another function that the vet has is to ensure that animals are rested prior to slaughter. After traveling for upward of twenty hours from farms as far away as Namibia, 965 kilometers (600 miles) or more, South African law says that the animals must be rested and fed in clean, sheltered pens. If an animal is sent to slaughter, and that animal is heavily pregnant, the vet will take care that the animal is pulled out of the slaughter lines and is allowed to have her young in a clean, safe environment. Vets see to it that this place of death is as humane as it possibly can be.

There were five vets working at the abattoir in Cape Town at that time, and there were five different jobs to do; each week we would rotate duties. There was meat inspection at the cattle line, at the sheep line, at the pig line, and at the horse line, and there was control of the pens.

There were pens housing animals that had just been unloaded from trucks, animals that had been rested and were now fit for slaughter, pregnant animals as well as animals that had given birth, and animals that required emergency slaughter. These animals may have been very sick or injured in transit, and the slaughter process was instituted immediately for humane reasons. There were also the ramps used for unloading animals that had just arrived at the abattoir, whether by road or train. The outside duty vet also had access to a powerful rifle and was authorized to use the rifle to shoot an animal that may have escaped or was judged to be a danger to personnel, other animals, and itself.

One week it was my turn on outside duty. I did not wish to look like Wild Bill Hickok of the Wild West when I walked around the facility, so I left the rifle in the gun safe. I had hardly ever had a problem, and certainly I had not yet been required to shoot an animal. In any case, I was a pathetic shot. Ever since the navy, where I had received firearms training, I shut my eyes each time the gun went off. Obviously, this is not conducive to hitting a target with any degree of certainty and reliability. Besides, I didn't want to walk around the abattoir with a rifle slung under my arm looking like the great white hunter, because that was the last thing I felt I was.

During that week, a railway train from what was then South West Africa (now called Namibia) had arrived at the rail siding, and the abattoir staff started to offload Brahman cattle from the trucks. These animals were reared primarily on large farms in rural settings, and they had hardly ever seen humans. They were wild in the true sense of the word and posed a real danger to the staff. The animals were herded from the trucks into chutes that took them to the pens in which they were to be housed. The chutes were steel and tall enough to ensure that none of them escaped, and the pens that they were going to be housed in had sides high enough to prevent their escape. Of course, the best laid plans . . .

As bad luck would have it, one of these wild bulls escaped. As usual, no one knew how it escaped, and of course it was no one's fault. I chuckled quietly to myself; how could anyone be blamed for what must have been a divine act? Little did I realize how soon my quiet mirth would turn to abject terror.

One of the staff employed to unload animals from the trains came running over to me, shouting and screaming that the bull was causing havoc on the railway tracks. Because I had never had cause to use the rifle, the last thing on my mind was fetching it. I ran over to the railway tracks with the worker and was presented with quite a sight. The rest of the animals had all been offloaded from the train, and all the staff had sought shelter from the storm that was this wild Brahman bull. Luckily, it had escaped onto the tracks, because the tracks were fenced in for safety by a high wire mesh fence on either side. This meant that the animal was effectively penned in. There were gates on each end of this "pen." Our plan was to enter the first gate and chase the bull to the gate at the other end, which led to a large holding pen. I managed to get a few of the workers to assist me and briefed them. They were to run ahead to the far gate and hide behind it, while I would enter the near gate waving my jacket, thereby frightening the bull toward the other gate. Based on previous experience, we felt that the plan would work. It was very unlikely that this bull would not run from noisy humans. It was even more unlikely that the bull would attack, so I felt comparatively safe. It has always amazed me that a 1,000-pound animal will run away from a 200-pound rather puny human being, but that is just what happens all the time. Well, almost all the time.

I waited until the staff were in position at the far gate, and then, with my heart thumping away and with a very dry mouth, I opened the near gate and walked cautiously toward the bull. It stood motionless for a while, just long enough for me to get fairly far along the tracks until I passed the point of no return. I had my jacket in my hand, and I started waving it and making lots of noise. I wanted to get this over with as soon as possible, because I really was frightened. Contrary to plan, and to my horror, the bull started to move toward me. I redoubled my efforts at waving and shouting, but this seemed to only spur the bull into a headlong gallop. I must have had all of three or four seconds to get the hell out of the way. I lunged for the fence and grabbed the barbed wire strands at the top, completely oblivious to any pain. Somehow, I managed to get a good grip with one hand and pulled myself out of the way of this rampaging animal. It careened past me at the speed of a runaway freight train, while I scrambled over the fence. The workers ran out of the far gate, and the others shut the near gate. We were back to square one, with the bull on the railway lines and us on the outside.

I took stock of my situation. I was now bleeding and really had been given an enormous fright. The bull was rampaging up and down the track and was in great danger of breaking a leg or, worse, getting out and really hurting someone. A decision had to be made. I decided that it was time to fetch the rifle. I asked the workers to keep all the gates closed and to stand clear of the fence. By now, the hullabaloo had attracted quite a few spectators, and the situation was deteriorating. The more people who were about, the bigger the chance of injury. Time was not on my side. I ran back to the office where the gun safe was kept and dialed in the combination. I grabbed the rifle and the magazine and ran back to the track. When I returned, there were even more of the staff standing round, and nothing I could do or say would make them leave. The mob of people seemed to inflame the bull even more, and it was now bellowing and stamping and charging the fence. It was entirely possible that it would break through the wire fence and maim or even kill the bystanders. I did not have a choice. To my utter dismay, I realized I would have to shoot the bull.

Since I was not the best shot in the world, and shooting through the fence might hit someone on the other side, my only option was to enter at the far gate and somehow take a shot at the bull and hope for the best. If I think back on this decision, in the cold light of day, I accept that at the time I must have taken leave of my senses. I should at least have asked someone else who was a reliable shot to use the rifle. I plead insanity at the time.

With great trepidation, I made my way to the far gate and entered the track holding the rifle at high port. I stood in the middle of the tracks, raised the rifle to my shoulder, and took aim. The bull must have been about 200 meters (220 yards) from me. He saw me standing there and started once again to move toward me, first at a walk, then at a trot, then finally at the speed of an express train. There I was, staring down the barrel of the rifle, dry mouthed, sweaty palmed, and very scared. It didn't help that the staff lining the fences were cheering and shouting. This was great sport to them.

This time, however, survival instincts took over, and within an instant my shaking stopped: It was kill or be killed. I looked down the barrel of the rifle as the bull came toward me, until it completely filled my vision. I squeezed the trigger, keeping both eyes wide open. The rifle shot exploded and slammed into the bull exactly where I had aimed. The bull careened and then crumpled up in a heap about 5 meters (5 yards) from where I stood, dead on arrival.

I expected to collapse in a heap of nerves, but amazingly another very surprising emotion took hold of me. I am not a hunter, and I abhor the senseless killing of animals in the name of sport. Yet, standing there, just having survived an all-out assault by a bull that was intent on killing me, I was suddenly overtaken by an atavistic urge to place one foot on my victim and beat my chest in triumph. Needless to say, I did not do this, but the urge was very strong at the time. I could understand how our primitive ancestors must have felt when they successfully hunted and killed an animal.

The dead bull was swiftly loaded onto a trolley and taken to the slaughter lines, where it was processed and turned into meat and by-products. I was glad to know that nothing of this bull would go to waste. My belief is that if a life is sacrificed, then at least we should respect that life by using the products rendered.

I put in my time at the abattoir and left after one year and went full-time into private practice. I like to think that I am a healer and a fixer, not a killer. The death that surrounds an abattoir eventually got to me. I have many memories and experiences from this time, but the memory of how I shot the bull is the one that is strongest and will stay with me until my dying day.

CHAPTER 5

Monkey Business

FOR MOST OF MY TWENTY-FIVE YEARS AS A VET, I HAVE TREATED species I am familiar with, mainly dogs and cats and a few small mammals like hamsters thrown in every now and again. I have, however, never shied away from other species, so my cumulative experience has been broad. Sometimes circumstances prevail, and I am forced into unexplored territory. The road less walked. The path less traveled. I remember the words of one of our professors at veterinary school. He said, "The similarities between species are vast; the differences are few and far between." It is so when treating different species. Basic rules apply, and if you obey them and are diligent, then you will most likely do a reasonable job.

One day while waiting for my next patient at my practice in Cape Town, my receptionist came and told me she had made an appointment for me to see a squirrel monkey. The owners (two women) were very worried because the monkey had been salivating profusely, and they were on their way to our office momentarily.

Oh no, I thought to myself and groaned. I had not treated a monkey for fifteen years, and I was not sure where to even start my examination process. I was not even familiar with how to handle or restrain a monkey. When the owners arrive, I thought, I'll send them elsewhere. I'll call some colleagues and find out who can see their pet.

The first thing these two distressed ladies did was to thank me profusely for consenting to see their monkey. They told me that they had called more than twenty vets, and each and every one had told them what I was going to tell them: Take the monkey elsewhere. Their good fortune was that my receptionist had taken the call and booked them without consulting with me first. Well, the monkey was now in my waiting room, and I was clearly, if uncomfortably, their last resort. I thought that a quick look would certainly not do much harm. With this in mind, I ushered them into the consulting room.

Monty was the cutest little guy. He was a squirrel monkey and weighed under a kilogram (2 pounds). His tiny face was endearing, and his eyes, like all new world primates, faced forward. He gazed out of his traveling cage with what appeared to be innate intelligence, and his little hands clutched at the bars of his cage. Once his owners set the cage down, they put their fingers in through the bars, and Monty grabbed a finger with each of his hands and held on for dear life as though the fingers represented familiarity and security.

I had a look through the bars to try to gauge the severity of the problem. One of the owners, Mrs. Daley, told me that Monty was off his food and was salivating profusely. I noted that he was completely wet around his muzzle, and he was in fact drooling a bit. But before I went forward, I needed help with a diagnosis and a plan of action.

About fifteen years prior, I had a friend, Jurgen Seier, who headed the primate unit at the Medical Research Council in Cape Town. I wondered if he was still around. He would at least be able to steer me in the right direction. I took the telephone book and looked up the surname, and there, sure enough, was a listing for J. Seier at the address I remembered. A female voice answered my call. I guessed it was his wife and asked sheepishly if she remembered me. With a burst of enthusiasm, she said she had recently read my book, *It's a Vet's Life*, and how thrilling it was to have me call them. Modest fame has its perks. She called Jurgen to the phone.

I spoke to him and told him my problem, as well as some of the symptoms I had seen during my brief observation of Monty. He gave me pointers about how to handle the little monkey. He also gave me a list of possible problems that could cause the symptoms I was seeing. The bottom line was that in order to examine him, I would have to sedate him deeply and even possibly anesthetize him. I had all the drugs I needed, and at least administering anesthesia was familiar work for me. I also had a chart giving me the accurate doses per body weight of animal. I explained all this to the owners, and without much hesitation, they gave me permission to go ahead.

I then asked Mrs. Daley to take him out so I could examine him properly before injecting him with the sedative. She opened the cage, and Monty jumped out and onto her shoulder. She grabbed his tail firmly so that he was forced to stay on her arm. As soon as I tried to examine him, however, he jumped onto my arm and scrabbled on to my shoulder. This was going to be tricky. I could see that Jurgen was correct. I would need to knock him out if I was going to get anywhere. I took out a small scale and weighed him. We did this by first weighing his traveling cage empty and then repeating the process with him inside. He weighed 940 grams (33 ounces). I calculated the amount of anesthetic I would need and drew the drug combination into one syringe. I then asked his owners to restrain him and wrap him in a towel, and I quickly administered the dose by injecting it into his rump.

As the effect of the drug took hold of this dear little fellow, he started to droop, and within the prescribed time he was lying on a warm towel fast asleep, looking like a hairy human infant. In repose he assumed the position of a curled-up sleeping child.

I lost no time in checking his vital signs, and when I was satisfied that his level of anesthesia was safe and stable, I turned to look in the most obvious place to diagnose why he was salivating so heavily. I began to prod around his mouth.

Now, a squirrel monkey's mouth is full of razor-sharp teeth, and it is so small that it is really difficult to examine. I had my magnifying jeweler's loupe handy and put this on to get a better look. I also used my operating lights to make sure that there was maximum light to work by. What I found in his mouth could certainly explain all his symptoms.

It turns out he had quite severe dental tartar. This is a hard concrete-like substance that coats the teeth of many animals to a greater or lesser extent. Its presence is abnormal and denotes dental and gum disease. This condition does not occur that commonly in wild animals but seems to be a blight of domestication. Domestic dogs and cats have tartar, wild ones or feral ones don't. I am not certain about monkeys, but I venture to guess that the same applies, and this problem may have been caused by a domestic diet. Certainly, a lot of my dental work involves removing dental tartar from my patients.

We always do this under general anesthetic, and we use a special ultrasonic instrument that cracks the tartar safely off the teeth. Once this is done, we wash out our patients' mouths to remove the loosened tartar. We then use a high-speed dental polisher to clean the teeth. After this we usually attend to the gums, which can be badly infected as well. This is exactly what I did with Monty. I had to wedge his mouth open with a small homemade gag. I then scaled all his teeth with my dental scaler. I spent a few moments going over his very impressive set of teeth until I was satisfied that all the tartar had been removed. I noted that he also had severe gingivitis. This is gum inflammation and manifests as a very red and sometimes bleeding gum line, where the gum and the tooth meet. I cleaned his gums with a diluted antiseptic. Once the teeth are scaled, polished, and cleaned, and pockets of infection under the gum margin are dealt with, the gingivitis usually clears up. There are also drugs that I use to assist with treating gingivitis. After this was done, I once again had a careful look at all his teeth, peering into his mouth through my loupe. I noticed that one of his teeth was broken and that the live pulp was visible. The tooth had discolored and looked dead. This tooth would have to come out. I took my dental extractors and ever so gently started to work the bad tooth loose. I really had to be extra careful because it is easy to fracture the jaw of a chap as small as Monty if one is overenthusiastic in the extraction process. My strength relative to the strength of his jawbone was no contest, so I had to be very gentle.

Monty was still asleep, but over the last few moments of the procedure, he had lightened up a bit. I was not unduly worried because I was nearly finished. We were not prepared, however, for the little shriek of pain that he made when his tooth came out. It gave us all a great start, but better a shriek from a live patient than silence from a dead one. Luckily, in the right hands anesthesia is very safe, and the incidence of problems is so low that one can almost guarantee survival. I was now finished, and Monty was safely coming around. All I needed to do was inject him with covering antibiotics and an anti-inflammatory. It crossed my mind that possibly I should administer some fluids by injecting warm saline into his abdomen, a method called intraperitoneal (IP) fluid administration, but I felt that the procedure had been reasonably quick, and on balance he would be okay. He also showed no signs of dehydration.

I kept him at my clinic for another half hour, and once I was satisfied that he was actually waking up, I allowed the owners to take him home. I gave them my phone number and asked them to call me later that night to inform me of his progress. They did call me to let me know that he was awake but still a bit groggy, and they were keeping him in his cage for the night. I told them that I wanted a further report the next day. I wanted to know that he was eating and drinking. If he was, then my diagnosis and treatment were on the money, but if not, then I had plan B. This would be to anesthetize him again and somehow find a vein in his tiny arm and drip him with fluids. I would then take blood to run though our laboratory. There was always the possibility that he had an organic disease that was the cause of the problem, and the tartar and bad tooth were red herrings. Alternatively, the tooth could be the primary problem, but due to infection, he had become systemically infected and needed more vigorous treatment.

I have a saying I apply to my practice when diagnosing a problem: When you hear hooves, think of horses. If you have a clinical sign, and there is a problem that fits the sign, then this is more than likely the cause. If this had been a dog or a cat with the same set of symptoms, namely, salivation and loss of appetite, and I had found the animal's teeth in the state I found Monty's, I would have been happy to make the same diagnosis.

I believe that this approach is called Occam's razor. It is a principle attributed to a fourteenth-century English logician and Franciscan friar, William of Ockham. The principle states that the explanation of any phenomenon should make as few assumptions as possible, eliminating those that make no difference in the observable predictions of the explanatory hypothesis or theory. In other words, if you hear hooves, think of horses.

The next day dawned, and I was up early with anticipation. Would Monty be well, eating and drinking as before, or would we need plan B?

Mrs. Daley called to tell me that Monty had in fact taken a small sip of water, but he was still groggy and not reacting normally. Once again I was not unduly worried and asked her to bring him in for examination. She did this, and what I saw was a little monkey who seemed to appear normal, if a trifle unsteady on his feet. Well, domestic animals can take twenty-four hours to shake off the effects of anesthesia, and I had attended to Monty at five o'clock the previous evening, so it was only about fifteen hours since he was anesthetized. I made a clinical assumption that he was okay, considering the time frame, and once again decided to wait a bit. What I also did, though, was to find out some further information about monkeys. I first put a call through to Peter Rogers, my wildlife vet friend in Hoedspruit, and after giving him the facts of the case, I listened to what he had to tell me. He said that these little creatures suffer from pain that can cause them to stop eating and that they can dehydrate very quickly. He also told me they become hypoglycemic when their blood sugar falls too low if they don't eat, and Monty had now not eaten for two days. After speaking to him, alarm bells started ringing, and I felt less at ease. I then called another colleague, David Huchzermeyer, in Leydenberg. David is a fish expert, but he has also had experience treating and caring for monkeys. He reiterated what Peter had to say. In addition, David mentioned treating Monty with magnetic pulse therapy. My wife, Kathy, had a Bemer unit, a special bioelectric magnetic field therapy mat. I was thrilled that Kathy had it and asked her if it was okay to use the Bemer on Monty. She said, "With pleasure."

I sent Monty home again because, even though I was vaguely concerned, if I was going to treat him again, I would have to once again anesthetize him, and this was not a great idea right now. Sending him home was a gamble after hearing what my two friends had said, but when I looked at him and noted that he was awake and had made some attempts at eating, I felt that we really needed to give him a bit more time. Once again Mrs. Daley took him home, and even though the next day was Sunday, I asked her to call me with a report early in the morning.

I received her message at eight o'clock the next day. She told me that Monty was really not well. He was lying in his cage and showing no signs of wanting to eat or drink. He had difficulty in rising and was unresponsive to their calls. I knew we had to do something now, or we would lose him. Yesterday's gamble had not paid off, and now Monty was in serious trouble.

I scheduled a meeting with her for later that day and went to open the practice at the appointed time. I had brought Kathy's Bemer with me and was prepared to try anything. Mrs. Daley arrived and brought the cage into the prep room, and what I saw shocked me. Monty had deteriorated dramatically. He was lying on a towel and really looked like he was dying. His eyes were open, but he was unresponsive, and he was panting and breathing with difficulty. No matter how often we called him, he just lay still. When offered a finger, he gently held it for security. This poor little creature was now in serious trouble, and I felt simply awful that I had not intervened earlier. How had he deteriorated so quickly? Why had I not been more proactive yesterday?

Mrs. Daley said that her family had discussed the situation, and they did not want to see Monty suffer. They were prepared to put him to sleep. I said that he was still alive (if only barely), and treating him was worth a try. Where there is life, there is still hope. They gave me permission to carry on, and I swung into action. I prepared 100 milliliters (about 3 fluid ounces) of fluids, took a butterfly needle, pierced his abdomen, and injected the fluids using the IP route. I had added dextrose to the fluids in case his blood sugar was too low. After administering the fluids this way, I injected antibiotics and a shock dose of steroids into his rump, then placed him on the Bemer. I was heartbroken to see this little creature lying there dying. He was simply much too human for my liking. After giving him the treatment, he certainly did not seem any better. We stood looking at him for about a half hour and discussed the various options and permutations. Eventually we decided to send Monty home with his owners, who would watch him continuously. I asked Mrs. Daley to come to my house that evening at six o'clock for a repeat treatment.

At the appointed time, they arrived, and once again I examined Monty. There was not much difference. I repeated the treatment by once again administering IP fluids, antibiotics, and anti-inflammatories and placing him on the Bemer again. David had advised five or six treatments, each one about four to six hours apart. I really did not hold out much hope. Monty was to all intents and purposes dying. How had things gone so wrong so quickly? What made me feel even worse was that his owners were so grateful to me for trying to treat him. I wished that the outcome was going to be different. After I had finished, I discussed the probable outcome with Mrs. Daley. We were all very somber. I had done all I could, and I told them to take him home and make him comfortable.

Over the last eight hours, I had given him 15 percent of his body weight in fluids and had dosed him with what I felt were appropriate drugs; too little, too late. Well, at least he would die at home. He was semi-comatose, and I felt that the end would be quick and his suffering kept to a minimum.

The next morning I went to my favorite coffee shop, where I consoled myself with a morning cup. Ah well, I had tried my best. I was just finishing my coffee when my phone went off, and I saw that it was Mrs. Daley's phone number. She was obviously calling to tell me of his passing. I almost did not want to take the call, but reluctantly I did.

To my surprise, when she said hello, her voice sounded happy. It took me a full minute to realize what she was saying. She said that it was a miracle. Monty had made a full recovery and was up and about in his cage and eating and drinking.

Besides being overjoyed, I was flabbergasted. How was this possible? Last night at six o'clock, Monty was about to take his last breath. Recoveries like these just don't happen, or do they? I asked her to bring Monty round immediately and quickly paid for my coffee and shot off to the practice to await their arrival.

Monty looked as good as she said he did. Here was a vigorous, cheeky little monkey who was a far cry from the dying patient of yesterday. Despite knowing that the treatment I had given him yesterday was good, I never imagined such a dramatic recovery.

Over the next two days, Mrs. Daley brought Monty back twice a day for Bemer therapy, and he never looked back. His recovery, although miraculous, was uneventful. He was eating and drinking, and it was just thrilling to see this.

When he got sick initially, he was ten years old. As a species, his kind live in excess of twenty years, so with a little bit of luck, he still had half his life ahead of him. Others had turned these kind people down, and even though I was their last resort, I had succeeded where others had not even bothered to try. Fools may rush in where angels fear to tread, but I was proud to have been the fool.

My wife ascribes his miraculous recovery to the Bemer, and who am I to argue?

Chapter 6

Cry Wolf

THE LEGACY OF APARTHEID, THAT INIQUITOUS POLITICAL SYSTEM THAT was the disease of South African society for nearly fifty years, manifests itself in places so strange that they sometimes defy imagination. For example, horses were specially bred by the South African Defence Force (SADF) that were highly suited to bush conditions, and these animals were used by a mounted unit to hunt "freedom fighters." Vast tracts of prime "game reserve" land became privately owned by people given preferential treatment for their allegiance to the government of the time.

In the 1960s, during the height of the apartheid government's power, the SADF purchased approximately two hundred wolves from the United States. At the time, there were border wars, and freedom fighters affiliated to the then banned African National Congress (ANC) were infiltrating the border with the intention of committing so-called acts of terror. The idea was to defend the Old South Africa using the talents of these amazing animals. The plan was to breed a wolf hybrid known as a "wolf dog," whose sense of smell and ability to track would be greatly enhanced, and use their enhanced senses to track down freedom fighters as they attempted to infiltrate the country. Wolf hybrids are very difficult to train, and despite endless efforts, the military failed to get the wolves and the artificially bred wolf dogs to respond to commands. The project was eventually shelved. The wolves and the wolf hybrids bred during the program were given away to the public whenever possible or euthanized. The breeding of wolf hybrids was continued by a few enthusiasts, who themselves tried to cross these magnificent animals with German shepherds, malamutes, or Siberian huskies.

These hybrids do not make good pets, as they require a lot of attention, and when they reach adulthood, they can become very dominant and dangerous. Most owners sadly end up giving them away or euthanizing them once this fact is realized.

There was, however, a small group of enthusiasts who continued to breed these magnificent creatures. A few animals trickled onto the marketplace due to their efforts, and over the last nearly forty years, a number of generations of the "wolf dogs" have appeared. They are true to type and still display the behavior that has all at once made them so desirable but so unpredictable and possibly dangerous. The enthusiasts who breed these animals keep records, and they try to cross the wolf dogs back with animals that have more pure wolf blood in them. Most of these animals have a pedigree, and it is possible to calculate just what percentage of North American timber wolf there is in each one.

About nine years ago, a male wolf dog was born to hybrid parents. His human owners named him Hoka, an anglicized version of Heyeokah, a native North American term for a shape-shifter. Hoka was approximately 87 percent North American timber wolf. He was owned by people who eventually immigrated to the United States, and they could not take him with them. If a suitable home could not be found, Hoka would be destroyed. Due to very specific requirements associated with wolf hybrids, Hoka could not go to just any suburban home. Wolf hybrids are "one person" animals, and that person must be an adult. They do not have a great reputation with children, and under no circumstances should children be left alone with these animals. The new owner would have to be strong-willed enough so that Hoka accepted his authority as the alpha male of the pack. Linton Pope owned a 500-hectare (1,235-acre) farm in Cedarburg, and after discussions with the owners, he offered to give Hoka a home in the mountains.

Adopting an adult wolf hybrid is an extremely difficult task because the "pack" has already been formed, and migrating from one pack to another is not a usual occurrence within wolf society. There was a lot of adapting needed by both Hoka and Linton. Hoka needed to accept a new leader in the pack. Linton would need to demonstrate that he had earned his place as the head of the pack, or Hoka would usurp the role of alpha male with disastrous consequences for Linton. Many times Hoka tested Linton's authority as they engaged in rough and tumble. But with patience, care, and love, Linton eventually won over this magnificent animal, and a happy calm descended on their newly formed pack. Hoka had a large camp to roam in and had about as much freedom as possible. Life could not have been much better for him.

Wolves and wolf hybrids are susceptible to many of the diseases domestic dogs get. This is where I came into the picture. I first encountered Linton when he called me for some advice about his wolf hybrid who appeared to be under the weather. I am not a great fan of long-distance diagnoses and treatment for many reasons. First, it is illegal, and second, a vet cannot make a proper assessment without examining the animal. But I knew how difficult it would be to get a semi-feral wolf, used to living on a large piece of land, to a vet's clinic, let alone my clinic 200 kilometers (124 miles) away. It would not be unreasonable to try to medicate from afar under these circumstances, and my empathy for the wolf and Linton won out. So, with Linton's intelligent questions and astute observation, we were able to treat Hoka over the phone with a modicum of success.

Linton called me one afternoon with a set of symptoms that had me worried. There appeared to be a creeping lameness associated with Hoka's hind legs. He seemed to be progressively getting weaker, and he was also having difficulty in walking and keeping his balance (ataxia). I questioned Linton carefully and asked him to make specific observations to get some clue as to what was going on. I really had to scratch my head to come up with a plausible explanation. I wanted to help, but I also wanted to avoid having Linton make the three-and-a-half-hour drive all the way from the Cedarburg Mountains into Cape Town with a semi-feral wolf hybrid.

One of my theories was that Hoka had been bitten by a tick, and the weakness and ataxia could be explained by tick bite fever. Another theory was that Hoka may have been bitten by a juvenile poisonous snake, and only a small amount of venom was injected—enough to make him sick, but not enough to kill him. Whatever the cause was, I knew that I had exhausted all obvious possibilities, and that this time I could not help unless Linton brought Hoka to town and I was able to examine him properly.

Now, this was a real problem. Hoka weighed over 60 kilograms (132 pounds) and was semi-feral. Linton could handle him, but that was about it. He was not amenable to being injected with a sedative, which is a basic starting point when handling wild or semi-feral animals. If they are not sedated, they present a clear and real danger to the person trying to examine them. After a lengthy discussion with Linton, we decided that the best plan was for Linton to rope Hoka and then get a muzzle on him. If we could do this, then we had a better than even chance of injecting him in his hindquarters with a sedative.

I called a number of friends of mine who worked with wildlife to get some information about sedating wolves, but no one knew what drug combinations to use or at what dose to use them. After trolling that marvelous source of information called the Internet, I discovered that a drug called xylazine worked well on wolves. I have this drug on my shelves, and its trade name is Chanazine in South Africa, Rompun in North America. It is a great sedative for dogs and cats, and used in combination with ketamine, it works well with wolves too, or so the Internet articles claimed. The articles also claimed that wolves often died under anesthesia. Boy, talk about Hobson's choice. Damned if you do, and damned if you don't. We had to sedate Hoka to make a diagnosis in order to save his life, but the very act of sedating him to make that diagnosis could cost him his life.

On the designated day, after my normal clinic hours, Linton arrived with Hoka in the backseat of his station wagon. From where I was standing, Hoka looked enormous and filled the back of the vehicle. Linton climbed out of the car, and we discussed the plan for the next few moments while Hoka looked on, not with the yellow eyes of a wolf, as I had expected, but with brown intelligent eyes that he must have inherited from his canine side. Linton would place a strong rope around Hoka's neck and lead him out of the car, then would try to muzzle Hoka. Once this was done, we would use the rope to pull Hoka's head up against a strong steel fence in front of my practice, and I would then sneak up from behind and, as swiftly as I could, inject the sedative into Hoka's hindquarters. At this point, I really wished for a dart gun but had to make do with a syringe.

Hoka climbed out of the car and walked toward me. This was going to be the only chance to examine him from afar and to see how he walked. I looked at him carefully in order to get a first impression. I noted that he had a lame front leg and seemed a bit wobbly, but what struck me most was that he walked with a wide-legged gait as if he had sore testicles. I thought, I wonder if this animal has sore balls. I was not aware then of just how significant a thought this was.

Hoka was not all that keen on our plan to immobilize him, but somehow, while both Linton and I were literally shaking with excitement, fear, and adrenaline, we managed to do exactly that. Hoka was so busy fighting the process that he did not realize that I was sneaking up quietly from behind. I had my syringe at the ready, and with one swift plunge, I injected the entire dose into his rump. He must have felt it, because his attention instantly switched to me, but it was too late. After taking a fraction of a second to discharge the syringe, I nimbly scuttled to the other side of the steel fence. Linton managed with soothing words to get Hoka to stop leaping around. Hoka settled down within a minute or so, and Linton was able to scratch his head. We were not brave enough just yet to remove the muzzle. Within five minutes, Hoka started to wobble and then vomited quite a large amount of food through the muzzle, which, fortunately, was designed for this eventuality. I was relieved when I saw this. If an animal has eaten before the drug is injected, it will make him vomit, thus purging his stomach and making the anesthetic a bit safer. I felt that this would now be a great time to move him inside, and we used the rope to guide him to my prep room, the heart of the practice, where all procedures are done. Hoka made it just in time, because as soon as he got there, he collapsed to the floor. Although he was deeply sedated, he was still conscious and muzzled. We still had to be very careful, because a sudden movement or noise could frighten him, and he might snap and do a lot of damage.

I decided that it would be wise to use anesthetic gas and a mask to deliver it. This way we could induce full general anesthesia to do my investigation. We wheeled the anesthetic trolley over to where he lay, and I switched on the gas and oxygen, then gave the mask to Linton to place over Hoka's snout. By now he was so drugged that we were able to remove the muzzle to make the masking process more effective. We kept the gas flowing for about five minutes, and in that time, Hoka became fully anesthetized. Once he was in surgical anesthesia, I intubated him. This entailed placing a tube into his windpipe, or trachea, and allowed me to put him properly on the gas. I attached a pulse oximeter to him. This is an instrument that would enable us to monitor his heart, the oxygenation of his blood, and other vital signs. We were thus able to further safeguard the anesthetic.

The first thing I then did, once I had made sure that my patient was safe and stable, was a blood smear to check for tick bite fever and also to look at the quality and quantity of red cells, the type and distribution of white cells, and a whole host of other useful diagnostic information. I made my blood film from a drop of blood taken from his ear, which I examined under a microscope. Even though this was my first wolf patient, I felt that I was in familiar territory—his blood had all the characteristics of a domestic dog. There were no signs of tick bite fever, but there was evidence of inflammation or infection. My next thought turned to what I had seen when Hoka stepped out of the vehicle.

Very occasionally, you have a clinical hunch, and you get lucky if your hunch is proven correct by the first test you do. I had a hunch, once I had seen Hoka, that he may have a prostate problem. My next step, after the blood smear, was to feel his prostate by doing a rectal examination on him.

By reaching into his rectum as far as I could go with a gloved hand, and by lifting his abdominal organs up to my outstretched gloved finger with my free hand palpating his abdomen, I was able to feel what was clearly a much enlarged prostate gland. If this diagnosis was correct, it could explain all the clinical symptoms we had noted so far. I moved Hoka to my X-ray room and took a picture. I then used an ultrasound machine to scan his prostate. We quickly saw that Hoka's prostate, which should have been the size of a golf ball, was the size of two fists placed together. He also had a grossly distended bladder and a filled rectum that confirmed the diagnosis of a prostate problem. My initial thought that he "had sore balls" was closer to the mark than I could have hoped for. My diagnosis of prostatic hyperplasia was confirmed. The treatment of choice for this condition is to sterilize the animal. I spoke to Linton about this, and it was agreed that Hoka should be castrated. He was still under full general anesthesia, so we decided that there was no time like the present to do it. We placed Hoka in a special surgical cradle and positioned him so that he was lying on his back with his legs stretched out, thus exposing the area that we were going to operate on. My assistant prepped him for surgery by shaving and scrubbing the area, and we then sprayed antiseptic fluid onto the area and wheeled him into the operating theater.

Once there, Hoka was again linked to the anesthetic machine and the cardiac monitor, which emitted comforting beeps. With these reassuring sounds in my ears, I prepped myself for surgery. Castration means removing the testes, the main source of testosterone, a male hormone strongly linked to prostatic enlargement. Once accomplished, the male hormone levels drop dramatically, and the enlarged prostate shrinks to almost nothing. It is a very effective method of treating this problem in dogs, and I hoped it would work in this wolf dog as well. I sutured Hoka with dissolving material because I did not fancy the prospect of having to remove stitches from him, and I also wanted to spare Linton that task as well.

After the successful surgery, we decided that Linton should drive back to his farm before Hoka was fully awake. I felt that this would be the safest thing to do, so we transferred the still heavily sedated wolf to a large bed in the back of

Linton's station wagon and made him as comfortable as we could. Normally, I would never allow a sleeping patient out of my sight until he was fully awake, but this was an exceptional set of circumstances. The drive back was going to take over three and a half hours again, and Linton wanted to get going as soon as possible. I explained that he should make sure Hoka's tongue remained out of his mouth to protect his airway until he was fully awake, and with those final instructions, along with a set of antibiotic tablets to take care of any postop infection, Linton set out for home.

The journey was uneventful, as was Hoka's recovery from the surgery. Postoperative swelling was minimal, and Linton was able to administer the antibiotics by hiding them in meat that Hoka was fed.

Altogether, the procedure was simple and effective. It could have been a problem had Hoka chewed his wound and ripped out his stitches. Hoka's lameness disappeared within the prescribed time, and he returned to peak health within a few weeks of the operation. He resumed his life in the mountains, and peace and calm once again descended on Linton's household.

Hoka, because he was a hybrid, was essentially "man-made," just like any other breed of dog that we see as vets. Working with Linton reinforced for me how important it is for owners to choose a breed carefully to ensure that the dog fits into the family and surroundings that will become its home. Fortunately, Hoka and Linton seemed to be a perfect match.

But wolves and wolf hybrids are not suitable for the average dog lover. As pups, wolf hybrids are cute and appear gentle and lovable. This all changes when they mature into adult wolves at about age three, and that is why so many are given away or destroyed when this reality surfaces.

Wolf hybrids are potentially dangerous, particularly around children, despite the many owners who claim otherwise. There have been some incidents where children have lost their lives due to an innocent mistake, such as allowing a toddler to "play" with a wolf, or allowing a crawling infant to interact unattended with said "family pet." Contrary to popular belief, they do not make good watch dogs at all. These animals are absolutely not suited to an urban environment, and the breeding of them is now illegal throughout the United States.

CHAPTER 7

Sight for a Sore Eye

PREDATORS NEED BOTH OF THEIR EYES, NOTHING LESS, IN ORDER TO HUNT successfully. Their eyes are situated at the front of their heads so they can look forward toward their prey. This is called binocular stereoscopic vision. In contrast, an herbivore (often a prey animal) has eyes that are situated on either side of its head to gain as much peripheral vision as possible. In this way they can spot the hunter hunting them and maximize their escape opportunities.

There was a lioness called Mehlwane at the Thornybush game reserve situated just outside Hoedspruit, a small bushveld town on the western border of Kruger National Park in South Africa. She was the alpha female, the head of her pride. She initiated hunts, and very often she was the first lioness to actually hit the prey, taking it down and clamping her powerful jaws around its throat to suffocate it. She was pivotal in the hunting success of the pride. For a while, Mike Pieterse, the head game ranger on the reserve, had noticed that there was a black ring around Mehlwane's right eye. When lying quietly in the heat of the day grooming, she continually pawed the eye; it was generally half shut, with tears flowing out of it. Clearly, there was a problem.

It was decided that the wildlife vet, Peter Rogers, should be called in, and the lioness should be examined and, if possible, treated. Peter, after all, did most of the veterinary work at Thornybush. He managed to drive his vehicle to within a few meters of the pride, and with the aid of a pair of binoculars, he got a good look at Mehlwane's eye. His assessment was that there was a congenital problem known as an entropion. This is where the lower lid rolls in toward the cornea. There are small, fine hairs on the edge of the lower lid, and with the lid rolled in, these hairs continually scratch the surface of the cornea, causing a bad irritation called keratitis. This continues until the cornea becomes scarred and blue, thus rendering the eye useless. In the case of a lion, this condition could even lead to aggression toward people. Her hunting ability would become impaired, and she could go hungry and turn toward easier prey.

She needed surgery to fix the entropion. Although Peter had performed the surgery on a dog once or twice, he found himself in unfamiliar territory. He called me and asked if I had done this sort of work before. I replied that I was well versed in the surgery, having performed the operation many times on both dogs and cats. Kathy and I were then invited to come to Hoedspruit, and I would assist in the surgery. This was an invitation I just could not refuse.

I had been thinking about putting a TV series together that would extol the virtues of my colleagues throughout South Africa and the amazing work they did with wildlife. I managed to attract some sponsors, and with the money I obtained, we would be able to film this bush operation on Mehlwane. Going into the bush and working with wildlife made me realize just how skilled small animal vets have to be. We operate on animals as tiny as a kitten weighing a few hundred grams. We manage to inject into veins almost as small as a single hair on your head. Operating on a lion would be no problem, provided that someone with experience handled the dart gun needed to administer the anesthetic. I knew full well that my skills with a rifle were not great, and the fluke shot that had killed the bull did not qualify me to dart a lion just yet. The big difference was that we could not just grab the lion's paw and inject it. This had to be done from a distance that was safe enough to ensure that we were not eaten in the process.

Kathy and I and a team consisting of a cameraman, a sound man, and director Dianne Lucas flew into Hoedspruit. We hired a Kombi (Volkswagen bus) and made our way to the Thornybush reserve. Johan Van Eeden, the reserve's general manager, met us there. He ushered us into the beautiful lounge in the lodge, where we were greeted with refreshments served by white-gloved staff. Talk about back to the colonies! We had the feeling that we had been transported back one hundred years to when the British empire still thrived, and the great white hunters of old were lords of all they saw. This is the experience one gets from the top private game reserves in southern Africa. It is designed to make guests feel special, and we certainly did.

By the time we had settled into our rooms, it was midafternoon. It was too hot to go for a game drive, so we decided to have a swim in the lodge pool. We all met there and cooled off for a while. Once refreshed, we changed into light summer clothing and met under the thatched roof of the lodge patio. Close to four o'clock that afternoon, we were served tea. This was yet another example of Thornybush hospitality. I could see from the spread we were offered that we were in for a fat time. The word *diet* does not exist in lodge vocabulary. There were cream cakes, muffins, cucumber sandwiches, and many other delicacies. We were warned, however, by Johan that dinner would be served at seven thirty, so we had better save some space.

Once tea was cleared away, we had the opportunity to gaze over the river that flowed in front of the patio. On the large sandy bank were prints of all manner of game. We were told that the best time for viewing game from this vantage point was at night. The bank would be floodlit, and the animals did not seem to mind the artificial extra light.

Mike, the head ranger, came and told us that the game drive especially organized for us would leave in fifteen minutes. We went back to our rooms to fetch the various items we needed, such as binoculars, cameras, and bird guidebooks. We were hoping to see our feline patient that afternoon. The game vehicle was a 4×4 open truck with three rows of seats. There was also a tracker's seat on the left of the hood just above the front bumper. Our tracker's name was Ocean, and we were soon to discover just how sharp his eyes were.

We set off on dirt roads, and within the space of a few hundred meters, the lodge was completely hidden by the thick foliage. Mike was driving, and Ocean navigated. We saw bush and dirt; Ocean saw a veritable highway leading to the game animals whose tracks he spotted. We drove for a short while under his direction, then Mike slowed down because Ocean indicated that there were lions ahead. There, in the shade of a thorn tree, was a pride of female lions, and among these magnificent animals was our patient. We inched closer until I had a clear view of Mehlwane. The dark ring of tears was clearly visible around her right eye, and she was grooming and paying special attention to it. She repeatedly licked her paw, then rubbed the eye with the wet paw. She constantly blinked, and it was clear that she was in some discomfort. Mike told us that the word *Mehlwane* meant "the one with the eye." Apparently, she had been this way her entire life, and the trackers had given her the name. Well, tomorrow we hoped to fix her. Maybe her name would still be the same, but we hoped there would be nothing remarkable about her eye after we were finished with her.

The game drive took another hour, and as the sun was setting, we turned round and drove back to the lodge. We saw many other animals during that hour, but my mind was filled with a lioness with a very sore eye and the hope that I would be instrumental in helping to fix it tomorrow.

We arrived back at the lodge and were once again ushered to the thatched patio for cocktails. We were told that we did not have to dress formally for dinner and that it would be served in an outdoor dining room. Instead of a dinner bell, there was a set of African drums that the chef's assistant used to announce the dinner. We sat at tables covered by starched white linen with crystal glasses and silver cutlery. The waiters wore white uniforms and white gloves. The wine and the food were both superb, and the cigars we were offered at the end of the meal were of the highest quality. The bush experience at this level is very sophisticated and designed to evoke the rich splendor of colonial days. Thornybush succeeded outrageously in this. We decided to have as early a night as politeness would allow, so once dinner was finished and cigars had been extinguished, we headed for bed.

Our group was awakened at four thirty the next morning by a member of the staff politely knocking on our doors. Peter and I were going to perform the surgery that day, and he radioed us to tell us that we must go out and track down the lion. Once we located her spoor, we were to radio him, and he would make his way to us in his vehicle.

Mike, Ocean, and the other trackers and game rangers greeted us at the car park outside the lodge. With the Thornybush contingent and our party, including the film crew, we numbered more than ten people and filled two Land Rovers. We quickly loaded our gear onto the game vehicles and set off. I had a nervous knot in my stomach. All would be in vain if we did not find the lioness. But I needn't have worried. Ocean was an expert tracker. Within ten minutes he had spotted her spoor. I was hard-pressed to believe him, but he pointed to a thicket, and sure enough, there she was. I may have been skeptical before, but I was now convinced that a good tracker is essential in the bush.

We sat quietly in our Land Rover, observing Mehlwane and waiting for Peter. He arrived on time and quietly climbed out of his truck and took his equipment out. He assembled the dart gun and the dart, having estimated the lioness's weight and calculated the correct dose of anesthetic. He climbed into the front of our vehicle and from a distance of about 15 meters (50 feet) shot Mehlwane in the rump. The dart discharged its dose, and Peter started his stopwatch. It would take about six minutes for the drug to act. We sat tensely in the vehicle and waited. Although the dart's impact is quite painful, Mehlwane did not move very far. Within six minutes she was lying on her side and soundly asleep. The only trouble was that nine other large African lions surrounded her. How were we going to get rid of them? Mike and Ocean climbed out of the Land Rover, clapped their hands, and shouted. Amazingly, the lions took fright and ran away, like a herd of skittish antelope. Once they were gone, Peter and I walked to our sleeping patient to make sure she was stable and safe. This was the first time that we had the opportunity to physically examine the eye we were to operate on. We saw immediately that our diagnosis was correct and that she did have the entropion we suspected. It was a bad case and would require extensive remodeling to fix the problem.

When your pet dog or cat needs surgery, you take it to your vet's operating room. When an African lion needs surgery, you bring the operating room to the bush.

We decided that we would set up our operating station under the shade of a nearby tree. We took out a transporting mattress and rolled Mehlwane onto it. With the aid of six strong men, we carried the sleeping lioness to the designated site. She must have weighed about 250 kilograms (550 pounds), and all the muscle that we had was needed to move her.

Once under the tree, we set up our sterile environment. This may have been in the middle of the African bush, but no shortcuts were allowed. Mehlwane's sight depended on us, and we took this very seriously.

We left the mattress with the lioness on the ground and brought out our instruments. We would have to squat over her to perform the surgery. I would have preferred to work on a table, but it was not to be. We had the rangers and trackers assist with the transport of all the gear, while we prepared Mehlwane for surgery. We shaved the surgical site around her damaged eye, then scrubbed the skin surface with a sterilizing fluid. Peter and I put on sterile gowns and gloves and opened the sterile packs of instruments and drapes. We then draped off the surgical site. Once this was done, we were ready to start the operation.

The surgery to treat entropion is essentially a face-lift. There is too much skin forming the lower eyelid, and this extra skin allows the lid to roll inside. What the surgery entails is making an elliptical incision in the lower eyelid and removing this excess piece of skin. In the case of Mehlwane, the piece of skin was about 3 centimeters (1 inch) long by about 2 centimeters (¾ inch) wide. There is a muscle under the lid called the orbicularis oris muscle. This too needs to be transected, and a piece needs to be removed. Once this is done, the muscle defect is sutured closed, then the incision into the skin of the lower lid is closed. The vet estimates the size of the piece of skin and muscle to remove by cutting a small piece out, then pulling the edges of the wound together to see how the eye looks. By trial and error the correctly sized piece is removed. We removed a small piece of skin, pulled the lips of the wound closed, and realized that a bigger piece must be removed. After taking a second piece of skin, we were happy that we now had enough. We then had to suture the wound closed. We used a dissolving suture material because we didn't want to have to anesthetize Mehlwane again in ten days' time. In principle, the less one interferes with wildlife, the better.

The suture material was thick enough to resist the grooming efforts of a lioness. We also tied many more knots in each suture because Mehlwane would continue to groom the eye for the full ten days of healing. She might be able to undo a few of the surgical knots, but we tied so many on each suture that we felt sure that they would in fact hold the wound closed. This is a technique that Peter has developed over the years, and it works well. Very seldom do his surgical wounds break down. Once finished, we swabbed and cleaned the surgical site and mopped up the small amounts of blood. We injected the lioness with antibiotics and an anti-inflammatory that would also control pain. Many times lions fight and inflict nasty wounds on each other. They seem to have a very high threshold of pain, though. We felt that a small wound under her eye would hardly bother Mehlwane, but we administered the painkillers nonetheless.

During the entire surgery, we had a game ranger with a loaded rifle standing guard over us. Don't forget that we were in the African bush, and the smell of blood from the wound, as small as it was, could still attract the other lions back to their leader. Mike seemed to have developed a special affinity for this particular lioness, and he squatted with us for the entire surgery, anxiously looking on. Once finished, we all relaxed. I took Mehlwane's head in my hands and compared the surgically corrected eye to the normal one. It was remarkable. All evidence of the previous problem was gone. There was some postop swelling by now, but this would settle down, and then the full benefit of the surgery would be evident.

The drug we had used would keep her sleeping for the better part of the day, so we moved her into a special crate under a shady tree. General anesthesia disables a patient's ability to keep body temperature constant. If exposed to full sunlight, there is a real risk of hyperthermia and death. Our team of vets, trackers, and rangers grunted and sweated to move the large cat into the waiting crate. Just before we slid the gate closed, we had one last look at our patient to make sure all was well. We were going to return at six o'clock that evening to release her.

Unbelievably, it was still relatively early in the morning. It was now just after eight, and we had been up for four hours. We had worked hard and were now famished. I am amazed at just how hungry this sort of work can make you. Early mornings in the bush followed by hard surgical work with a liberal dose of adrenaline certainly leave me hungry. We climbed back into the Land Rover and headed for the lodge. We knew that shortly we would be tucking into a large breakfast and that our hunger would be satisfied.

The afternoon was spent in introspection. After the stress of the bush surgery, we needed some quiet time to fully appreciate what we had done. If the surgery was successful, and we were fairly sure it was, we would have made a real difference in our patient's life.

At about five o'clock we all gathered in the parking lot and loaded the gear into the Land Rover. It was time to release our patient. There was a quiet tenseness about us as we made our way to where we had left the crate and the sleeping lioness. The anesthetic that we had used was a drug called Zoletol. It was extremely safe, and we knew that our lioness would by now be wide awake. Releasing a wild lion from a flimsy wooden crate has its own set of dangers.

We arrived at the spot, and Peter and I quickly climbed down and walked over to the crate. We looked inside and could clearly see that Mehlwane was fully awake. She sat quietly inside and did not seem too stressed or unduly disturbed. I had expected her to growl or roar at us when she realized we were approaching the crate, but she gazed out through the small ventilation holes in silence.

Our plan was to stand on the crate and then slide the gate up and allow Mehlwane to run out. I must admit to being a bit nervous at the thought of standing a few inches above a wild lioness with only a flimsy piece of wood between her and me. I expressed my concern to Peter.

"Peter, are you sure that she's not going to try to seek revenge on us for what we've done to her?"

"Don't worry, Roy," Peter replied. "She will want to get as far away from us as quickly as possible."

We scrambled onto the box, and the rest of the crew climbed back into the Land Rover. The game rangers had their rifles at the ready, and Peter and I unclipped the lock on the gate of the crate. We gently slid it up and opened Mehlwane's way to freedom.

For a few moments she just crouched there, possibly confused by the sudden sunlight that flooded in. We were all frozen in our respective positions: us on the crate, the crew in the vehicle, the game rangers poised with their rifles, and the lioness in the crate.

Peter then stomped on the box, giving me a huge fright. He must have also startled Mehlwane, because she sprang out and ran off into the bush without even giving us a second glance. I am glad she was not aware of the tasty human morsels that were so close to her.

We had hidden a small digital camera just in front of the entrance to the crate and had activated it by remote control. We filmed the entire release in order to observe Mehlwane's eye. Once she had moved off, we retrieved the hidden camera, and with the aid of a monitor, we were able to view the footage. We were thrilled at the way the eye looked. During the few short moments when everyone was frozen, including Mehlwane, the hidden camera had a fantastic view of the lioness looking directly at it. Both of her eyes were wide open, and there was no indication of an entropion. The skin around the eye was black, but once the hair grew back and the sutures had dissolved, we were optimistic that we could call the surgery a success.

We left Thornybush the next day, satisfied that we had made a difference to our wild patient. But I somehow felt that the job was not completed. I was lucky enough to be called back to Hoedspruit a short while later, so within two weeks I had the opportunity to visit Thornybush and Mehlwane again. Mike agreed to take me to see her.

That afternoon we made our way to Thornybush in time for the game drive. We were taken through the bush once again with Ocean as tracker, and he found Mehlwane just as efficiently as before. She was lying in the shade grooming. She was not paying any special attention to her eye. I used a pair of binoculars to have a look at her eye and was both amazed and thrilled. The only sign of the previous problem was the black ring around it. This was due to the hair not having grown back and possibly to a lifetime of rubbing that eye and the surrounding skin. Both eyes were fully open, and the cornea of the eye we had fixed was clear and bright. She certainly had her binocular stereoscopic vision intact, and I could happily say that our alpha female was now back in business.

Chapter 8

Delinquent Elephant

TSHUKUDU IS A SPECIAL PLACE NEAR HOEDSPRUIT. IT IS A GAME RESERVE owned by the Sussen family and steeped in the old traditions of hospitality. One does not have to purchase designer safari clothing to fit in, but don't let that fool you, the food and accommodations are still superb. There is a special experience at Tshukudu that one does not ordinarily find in a game reserve. Here you can walk among wild animals. The Sussens have raised by hand wild animals that have become so used to humans that rangers and tourists are often accompanied by cheetahs, leopards, and an elephant or two. These animals are far from tame, however, and the rangers still carry rifles on their walks through the reserve. To date they have never had to use them, and I hope they will never need to.

My favorite animal in the African bush is the elephant. Only after I have spent time in their company do I feel that I have had my African experience. Both powerful and mythical, they embody Africa. They can be so loud that you can hear them from miles away, yet sometimes they are so silent that they can pass a short distance from you in thick bush without your even knowing it. You just don't know how large an African elephant is until you have the chance to stand next to him or, as I did once while an elephant was anesthetized, sit on him.

Tshukudu adopted two elephants from the Kruger culling program about fourteen years ago. Culling was a method used to control the elephant population in Kruger National Park at the time. The park had a "carrying capacity," which means that the land could support only a certain number of elephants. If this limit was exceeded, the population needed to be reduced by killing off the excess number of elephants. Unfortunately, culling was a method that was effective, although crude.

One of these elephants, Temba, was a male and the other a female. A few years after that, a wild elephant from one of the adjacent parks joined the small herd, and the female became pregnant from this interloper, who the owners called Slade, after a family acquaintance who ran off with someone else's wife.

The problem with culling elephants, besides the obvious one of killing a magnificent beast, is that one is sometimes left with baby elephants. These vulnerable little animals are then herded together, and those that survive the terror of the cull are sold to private reserves in the name of conservation. This is a very noble gesture, but the fallout over the years has been great. Orphaned elephants raised on reserves don't have the discipline of the herd to guide them in their adolescence, so their behavior becomes delinquent, remarkably like a human child who has not been properly socialized. The result is that by the time the elephant reaches puberty, between thirteen and fifteen years of age, we have a 3-ton animal behaving badly. This aberrant behavior often leads to a conflict of interest between the reserve and the elephant.

The male orphan named Temba had developed some bad habits. He tried to mate with several of the reserve's rhinos and in the process inadvertently killed three of them with his tusks. An elephant tusk with a 3-ton body behind it can slice through a rhino like a hot knife through butter. Temba had also learned how to use logs with his trunk to short-circuit the electric fence surrounding the lodge.

The results of an elephant breaking into places he should stay out of can be quite startling. Once Temba broke into the lodge pantry and ate over 100 kilograms (220 pounds) of canned pickles and glass jars of jam. He took the tins and glass jars, "cracked" them with his teeth, then swallowed the food—glass, cans, and all. He developed severe colic, and 3 tons of elephant with a sore tummy is not a pretty sight to behold. You can't just ask him to open his mouth and take his medicine like a good boy. My friend Peter Rogers once spent a busy night treating an elephant with a very sore tummy. Step one is immobilizing with an anesthetic dart; step two is starting an intravenous drip of 50 liters (53 quarts) of fluids; step three is giving a dosage of liquid paraffin (also called "opening medicine") to open the elephant's bowels; step four is administering the antidote to the anesthetic. Let me tell you, you don't want to be anywhere near an elephant that has been given "opening medicine."

On another occasion Temba freed the lions from their breeding enclosure. These lions gave the lodge staff and tourists quite a scare. Imagine coming out of your tent in the morning and being confronted by a large male lion looking for its breakfast.

The situation with Temba had deteriorated to the point that the elephant was becoming a daily nuisance, and something had to be done. Peter and I decided to collar Temba with a radio transmitter. His whereabouts would then be known at all times, and he could be monitored regularly. If he was found too close to the lodge or lion fences, then evasive action could be taken. A gentle "prodding" with the Land Rover could herd him away from the "danger zone" into a safer part of the reserve. If he was getting randy with the rhinos, we could chase him away from there as well. Hopefully, because elephants are such intelligent animals, Temba could be trained out of his bad habits by repetitive negative stimuli.

An elephant collar is not just an ordinary piece of equipment. It is made from industrial belting with a radio transmitter and a special battery. You can't just go up to an elephant and change the battery whenever it wears out, so you have to ensure that you provide a long-lasting one. The battery powering the transmitter has to be good for five years, and the collar must be strong enough to withstand the rigors of being worn by an adult elephant. It's also expensive and hard to fit, especially on a sleeping elephant.

Doctors and pharmacists in South Africa are licensed Act 101 practitioners, which means they can administer powerful sedatives, like M99. In the game world, veterinarians are the logical and legal practitioners. M99 is extremely dangerous to humans and should be handled by trained individuals only and with extreme caution. The dose used to knock down an elephant could in fact kill many hundreds of people. One small droplet on the mucous membranes of your mouth or your eye, and you will die unless an antidote is administered.

Peter invited me to join him in fitting the collar on Temba. Joining us were my wife and a film crew consisting of cameraman Clifford Bestall and a specialist sound man, Sebastian Dunn. Our group flew into Hoedspruit and drove to the Tshukudu game reserve, where we were met by the head game ranger, Ross Dunbar. After we settled in, Ross asked us if we wanted to go out on a game drive to examine our "patient" and get familiar with the surrounding terrain. We jumped at the chance of surveying the countryside and meeting the delinquent elephant.

Our first encounter with Temba was memorable. We drove down to the nearest water hole, and there, in plain view for all to see, were about ten white rhinos grazing. In the midst of this large gathering was Temba. His focus seemed to be on a female rhino with a calf at her side. As she tried to fend off his amorous attentions with her single horn, she aroused him all the more. The noise of horn and tusks clashing in the quiet of the African bush was like a clash of djembe drums.

The rhino also vocalized and snorted her indignation. Ross used the Land Rover to try to separate the courting couple. Once disturbed, Temba ambled off, and peace prevailed once more. This was a graphic demonstration of what the rangers would do in the future, once the elephant was collared. Once his whereabouts were easily ascertained, he could be monitored, and the same actions could be taken to break up the "party."

We drove around for a few hours that afternoon and experienced some of the many wonders that Tshukudu had to offer. We came across a cheetah that had just killed a small buck and was feeding on it. To my amazement, Ross stopped the Land Rover and climbed out. He then walked up to the cheetah and stroked her. He introduced her to us. This was Savannah, a hand-reared cheetah that lived on the reserve. She was wild enough to hunt for her food, yet she allowed us to stroke her while she ate. While we were petting her, she suddenly sat up and pricked her ears. We tried to hear what had disturbed her. Only when we were perfectly still did we hear lions in the distance. Cheetahs sometimes fall prey to lions, and Ross felt that it would be safer for Savannah to be taken back to the safety of the fenced area of the lodge. He radioed some of his colleagues, and they came out to attend to this. We then tried to find the lions, but it was getting dark, and eventually we had to give up. They were deep in the bush, and we just could not access the area by vehicle, and on foot would be too dangerous.

We retired early after a memorable dinner at the lodge. As I lay in my bed just before dawn, I heard the typical sounds of the Africa bush—the grunting of lions, the barking of jackals, and the stirrings of the lodge staff. Day was breaking, and the nocturnal animals that had been hunting and feeding at night would start to move toward their lairs to rest during the hot day. We, however, were just starting our workday. It seemed to me as though the whole process was a changing of the guard.

I had a tense feeling in the pit of my stomach. Today we were going to hunt the largest land mammal on earth—on foot, with only a dart gun. Admittedly, we would have Ross and his rifle with us, but only if things got out of hand. I never underestimated the danger of what we were doing. If the elephant decided to charge us instead of running off into the bush, there was always a chance that the ranger would have to fire to frighten him away. If he still came toward us, then the possibility of actually shooting him would be rapidly considered. Our safety was in the hands of Ross.

We met at the lodge at four thirty that morning for a quick breakfast, and Peter arrived shortly thereafter. Together we drove to where Temba was last seen. A tracker had spotted him before dawn, so we were able to find Temba without too much trouble. By this time the sun was up, and it was light enough to see quite easily. We stopped the vehicle about 200 meters (220 yards) from where the elephant was grazing peacefully and took out our equipment. Peter and I assembled the tranquilizing dart and loaded it into his dart gun. A dart gun used on elephants is fairly specialized in order to penetrate an elephant's thick skin. It's shaped like a rifle, and it fires the dart at a high velocity. The needle part of the dart is thick and long.

Ross, Peter, and I set out on foot to stalk the elephant. We had to come from downwind, or Temba would possibly take fright and run away. He was not used to being disturbed this early, and we were worried that he would suspect something was up. Elephants are remarkably intuitive creatures and are acutely aware of their surroundings. We were sure that if he saw or smelled us that early, he would move off into the thick bush, and this would make things much more difficult. We crept up on him quietly, using the bushes for cover. The ground was very soft underfoot, and our shoes were specially made for tracking. The soft soles hardly made a sound in the thick dust of the ground. The situation was very tense. I could imagine how hunters of old must have felt when stalking an animal. I had an adrenaline buzz, and my pulse was racing.

We were just about within shooting range when Temba suddenly looked directly at us. We had been spotted, and within a split second he would turn and bolt. Consummate professional that he is, Peter raised the dart gun to his shoulder and fired the dart into the elephant's hindquarters. Now, while an elephant's rump is as big as a barn, when it is moving away from you at 30 miles an hour, it is not an easy target.

Unlike me, who usually shuts my eyes tightly at the sound of a rifle's bang, Peter is an excellent shot, and his dart sped toward Temba and hit him exactly in the correct place, delivering its tranquilizing dose of M99. On impact the already startled elephant was given a further fright and accelerated off into dense bush. An elephant could cover a lot of ground in the ten minutes it took the drug to act, so it was imperative that we keep after Temba. If he lay too long in the hot sun, he could die of hyperthermia. If he collapsed on his chest, he could suffocate.

Ross's tracking team sped into action and followed Temba on foot. We followed too, albeit at a slower pace. The film crew and I were slowed up by our gear. We were in radio contact with the trackers, and within about ten minutes we were guided both by radio and with shouts to where the elephant lay. During that time we were in dense African bush, and once again I felt a strange unease. I had the distinct feeling that something was eyeing me and thinking "breakfast." We managed, however, to hike toward where the trackers had found Temba without encountering any other animals. From a distance of about 100 meters (110 yards), we could see that our elephant was lying in the shade and on his side. This could not have been better. We approached him rapidly, and as I got closer, I suddenly realized why this magnificent species was one of the "Big Five." Three thousand kilograms (6,600 pounds) of flesh and bone and muscle wrapped up in a very thick, gray, crusty skin is impressive, to say the least.

They are not called pachyderms for nothing. The word means "thick-skinned," and that is just what they are.

Peter and I used a small stick to ensure that the tip of Temba's trunk stayed open, thereby providing an unobstructed airway. Then we flapped his ear over his eye to protect it from the sun. While I was doing this, I could not help noticing the marvelous network of very large veins coursing through his ear. Some of these veins were as thick as my thumb. An elephant's ears are built-in air conditioners. All of an elephant's blood passes through his ears every few minutes, and when he flaps these large ears, he effectively cools the blood that is flowing through the ears at that time. The cooled blood then reenters his body, and in this way the elephant is able to cool himself very efficiently. While Temba was lying unconscious in the sun, we were able to use this remarkable system to cool him. We had a large can filled with water, and we doused his ears liberally while he lay there.

We applied some protective eye ointment to his eyes to prevent them from drying out. Sleeping patients lose their blink reflex, so the ointment was necessary to protect the eye from dust and flying insects.

It was my first close encounter with an unconscious elephant, so once Temba was secured, and we were satisfied that he was in no danger, I was able to step back and observe him. All the wonder and magic of being so close to one of Africa's true giants just overwhelmed me. When you stand next to a sleeping elephant, it is nearly as high as you are tall. Its abdomen is over 1½ meters (5 feet) in diameter at its largest point. The tusks on this particular elephant, while not enormous, were certainly long enough to do grievous bodily harm. Temba's skin was like the bark of a very old tree, hard and dry and crusted. The patterns on the skin were like mud that had dried up in a pan that had not had water for a long time. I opened his mouth and was able to examine his teeth, lips, and tongue. Believe it or not, this animal that eats thorn trees, bark, and other really hard material has a tongue as soft as velvet and teeth twice as big as a man's hand. Temba's lips were also very soft in comparison to the rest of his skin. The nails on his feet were as big as my hand, and the sole of his foot was tough enough to carry him through the African bush for up to eighty years. There is a thorn tree in the bushveld called a *sekelbos* in Afrikaans. The thorn of the sekelbos is long and sharp and very dangerous. If one of these thorns penetrates this giant's foot, then an abscess can ensue, and the animal is rendered lame and very vulnerable just from the effect of a tiny thorn. One of these thorns had in fact penetrated one of Temba's feet but had not yet caused an abscess. We removed the thorn, and I am sure that had he been able to, he would have thanked us.

The dart that delivered the anesthetic agent had a barb that allowed it to be "unscrewed" from the tough hide. Otherwise, it would have been a very difficult task to remove it. To complicate matters, the tip of the dart still had some M99 in it, enough to affect a person very badly. I removed the dart and placed a cover over the tip to safeguard us from the dangers of the drug. There were some routine procedures that we performed on the sleeping elephant. Peter has a philosophy: Anesthetizing game is not desirable, but when it needs to be done, it offers a good opportunity to deworm the animals and examine them, and, if there are any wounds or other abnormalities, treat them. With this in mind, we examined Temba thoroughly, looking for any obvious and not so obvious abnormalities. We injected a large dose of penicillin into him and gave him an elephant-size dose of injectable dewormer. Along with removing the thorn, we also treated some of the wounds on his skin topically. The final act after all this was to accomplish what we had set out to do, and that was to secure a tracking collar around his neck.

I took the collar from the Land Rover and placed it around my neck. It came down to below my feet. That meant that the elephant's neck girth was about 3 meters (10 feet). We slipped the collar under Temba's neck and laboriously pulled it through to the other side. It was then secured with a joining plate with four lockable bolts and nuts. Collaring an animal isn't easy. You have to judge how tight the collar should be on a recumbent animal. Too tight, and it will be uncomfortable; too loose, and it could slip off. If you're not careful, it can twist, and then you have a collar with the transmitter pressing into the animal's flesh. Over months this can cause serious wounds. With this in mind, we placed the collar on our elephant with just the right amount of tension and without a twist.

Once this last task was done, we injected Temba with the antidote to the tranquilizer. Elephants usually wake up within two minutes with no visible side effects from the drugging. The elephant's ear vein is used to inject the drug intravenously. I wished my small animal patients had such an easy vein to access. I was given the task of injecting the antidote, and once this was done, we removed the stick from Temba's trunk and flapped his ear back from covering his eye. We then walked a respectable distance from him and watched him wake up. I have to once again admit to butterflies in my stomach. This was a first for me, and I acknowledge that my lack of experience at the time caused me to be very nervous.

Temba flapped his ears and started to vocalize with rumbles that I felt deep in my chest. It was truly a primordial sound of the African continent. He rocked onto his chest and elevated himself onto his front feet while still lying on his hindquarters. Then, majestically, he rocked onto his hind legs and stood up. He appeared very relaxed and none the worse for his ordeal. He then ambled off into the bush as though nothing had happened. And in truth, nothing had, other than the fact that we had added a new fashion accessory to his otherwise drab gray attire.

We switched on our radio telemetry unit, and a strong beeping sound emitted from the receiving unit. When the directional aerial was pointed at Temba, the sound was strongest. If the aerial was pointed in the opposite direction, the sound was weakest. This way, using the aerial, we were able to track Temba and locate his whereabouts. From that time on, he would be routinely monitored, and if he strayed into an area that was off-limits, he would be herded away. We hoped that this new ability to track him would assist in controlling his behavior. We did not know it just then, but the very next day our system would be put to the test.

We had been working since five, and it was now just after eight in the morning. We had tracked an elephant, darted him, run through the bush, treated the elephant, and secured a collar on him, and we were now famished.

After lunch, I took the opportunity to explore the camp. There was a small kopje, a hillock, within safe walking distance from the lodge, and I took a slow stroll there and climbed to the top. The vista was superb. The foothills of the Drakensberg were visible in the distance; the mountains had a blue color to them. They were the gateway between the lowveld and the highveld. The vastness of Africa was visible from this elevated vantage point. The colors of the bush blended together to form a picture that is etched in my memory. The greens and browns of the dusty landscape dotted with stunted bush and trees and the vastness of the blue African sky are unforgettable. I had arranged a game drive for late in the afternoon, and between my walk and the drive, I took the opportunity to rest in my tent. When I finally went to bed for the night, I reveled in the sleep of the exhausted.

The next morning Ross woke me after sunrise, a very unusual event for me. I am usually up before the birds start tweeting. He was very excited and told us that Temba had been detected near the electric fence just outside the far end of the lodge. This was an area that he had damaged previously, and this piece of electric fence seemed to attract him. We were going to have the opportunity of testing our theory there and then. We used the tracking device to make sure that Temba was still where he was reported to be. Ross drove us to the location, and sure enough, there was Temba at it again. A rhino and her calf were standing next to the fence, and Temba already had a log in his trunk and was leaning on the fence with it. He was systematically pushing the fence with this log. Already there were some electric strands broken, and he was well on his way to gaining access to a prohibited area. Well, the moment of truth had arrived. Would we be able to scare off a 3-ton elephant with a 2-ton jeep? Don't forget that many a vehicle has been charged and flattened by an angry elephant, and the occupants did not always benefit from the attention. Ross gunned the engine, and we rolled slowly toward Temba with all our nerves atwitter. We were about 10 meters (33 feet) from him when Ross blew on the horn. With a sudden start, Temba tossed his log aside and ran off into the dense bush. We all breathed a great sigh of relief; we had been successful and had survived the first episode of Temba's reeducation. There was still a long road to travel, but our initial impression was that he was in fact trainable and with some effort would no longer damage fences. Only time would tell if we could divert his amorous attentions away from the rhino, but at least the reserve now had a method of determining his whereabouts, and we knew that he would move off from a vehicle and not charge it.

I look back on that trip with fond memories. It was March when we were there, a beautiful time for game reserves in South Africa. The days were still hot, but the nights became cool enough to sleep well. The bush was still green from summer rains, but because of grazing pressure, it had started to thin out, so we could see game through the bush.

Following this initial contact with Temba, I learned from Ross and Peter that Temba had "grown up," and that his delinquent behavior was now a thing of the past. He was moved from Tshukudu to a game reserve near a town called White River. He is now part of an elephant back safari conducted by the reserve. It is really thrilling to think I played a part in his reeducation. Maybe one day in the not too distant future I will make my way to White River and do an elephant back safari. I might even be lucky enough to ride Temba. Elephants have long memories. I wonder if Temba will remember me.

CHAPTER 9

The Gemsboks' New Home

MOVING WILD ANIMALS FROM PLACE TO PLACE IS BOTH A SCIENCE AND an art. Seemingly hardy animals easily succumb to stress and often die due to the trauma of capture and relocation. They need to be handled with great care and sensitivity to maximize their chances of survival. Some capture outfits chase their prey into capture nets, then physically manhandle the animals into vehicles. Needless to say, their success rate with these animals is rather low.

Game animals are susceptible to a disease called capture myopathy. This occurs when the animals are severely stressed due to the capture process. Lactic acid builds up in the muscles to the point that it becomes fatal. Other times the stressed animals are immune compromised and become sick and debilitated a few days after they are translocated. This is known as translocation disease. The best way to move animals is to involve veterinarians. These skilled professionals know how to tranquilize the game and move them in a way that maximizes their chances of survival. My skills at this were tested when Professor Dave Meltzer and I spoke about a particular gemsbok that had been relocated with its herd and was not faring well.

Professor Meltzer is the head of the wildlife department of the veterinary school at the University of Pretoria, commonly known as Onderstepoort. This is a world-class facility situated 16 kilometers (10 miles) north of Pretoria. The drive through Pretoria is always beautiful in spring. The city is known as Jacaranda City because of the profusion of beautiful trees lining the streets throughout the entire city. Toward the end of September, the purple jacaranda starts to bloom. This is usually the signal for students at the university to start poring over their books. If you are not studying when the jacaranda starts to bloom, then you risk failing the year, because you have left your studying until the very last moment. The veterinary school is staffed by some of the best vets on the African continent, and wherever vets who have qualified from this school go internationally, they are welcomed with open arms. Some of South Africa's most successful export commodities are its skilled graduates. They have carved an excellent name for themselves throughout the world wherever they work.

In the spring of 1998, I called Professor Meltzer to ask him if there were any interesting cases in or around Pretoria. My proposed TV series about being an African vet was still in its infancy, and my producer, George Mazarakis, and I were trying to film as many stories as possible in order to accumulate a library of them. Like all the clinical departments, the department that Meltzer heads up has an ambulatory clinic servicing the surrounding area, and if there are problems and clinical cases within a 50-kilometer (31-mile) range of the school, they usually send out a vet to treat the sick animals. These vets take students with them, and the experience gained via the ambulatory clinic is incredibly valuable.

Professor Meltzer told us that there was a herd of gemsbok that his clinic was currently dealing with, and he introduced us to Dr. Melvin Quan, a postgraduate veterinary student working toward a master's degree in wildlife medicine. Gemsboks are wonderful hoofed animals that grace the African plains. They are a sort of dun color and have dark brown and white markings on their faces. What really makes them stand out is their very impressive set of horns. These long scimitar-shaped weapons may be up to a meter (39 inches) long. Beware if the gemsbok tosses its head and you are in the way,

Melvin had been called out to a farm near Pretoria where a small gemsbok herd was having difficulty settling into their new environment. The farmer had purchased the animals from another location where the ecosystem was different from the one in which the animals now found themselves. One thing was for certain: A vet was not involved in their initial capture. It was not outside the realm of possibility that the animals had been herded into capture nets with no sedation or tranquilization. Animals handled this way often become entangled in the nets and are then wrestled down to the ground and manually hoisted into trucks. It seemed as though all the stress of capture and relocation was causing a problem for this particular herd. Their immunity had become depressed, and this rendered them susceptible to various diseases, as well as external and internal parasites. Our rapid intervention was necessary to help these animals survive.

We met Melvin around six o'clock in the morning. By the time we had loaded the gear into the vehicle, it was six thirty. We drove out to the game farm that was situated about 50 kilometers (31 miles) west of Pretoria. We drove through the outskirts of the city in September, which is early spring in South Africa. Rain usually comes to the bushveld in summer, and then the fields are transformed into lush green pastures bursting with life. For now, however, dust prevailed.

We arrived on the farm at about seven. It is crucial to work with animals in the cool of the morning rather than the heat of the day. When an animal is darted with most anesthetic agents, it loses its thermoregulatory mechanism, which is its ability to regulate its body temperature. Mammals are warm-blooded. This means that their body temperature is kept constant despite the external temperature. When the anesthetic agent dissociates the ability to keep the body temperature constant, the animal's temperature can soar, and death can ensue very quickly due to hyperthermia. Whether dealing with Mehlwane the lioness, Temba the elephant, or any other wild animals, we always applied the same basic rules. An animal that has just been darted can panic and run a good six minutes before the anesthetic takes effect. Believe me, sometimes trying to find a wild animal in the bush with a six-minute head start is impossible. These animals can then fall asleep in full sunlight, and only six minutes in the hot African sun is sufficient to kill.

Melvin assembled his dart gun, a crucial piece of equipment in any game capture. Some dart guns work with compressed air, some work with a small firing cap, and some even work as a blowpipe, with the operator using air expelled from his lungs to shoot the dart. Different systems have evolved to suit almost every occasion. On this occasion, Melvin had a compressed air dart gun that was accurate to about 50 meters (160 feet). Once this task was accomplished, we set off to find our sick gemsbok. The entire herd was mildly affected, but one particular animal had taken a turn for the worse, and we wanted to find him and see if we could treat him.

At the end of the dry season in September, the bush is reasonably sparse, and finding our sick patient was not too difficult. Melvin had his dart gun assembled and loaded with a syringe containing M99, the same drug used for elephants and rhinos. Now all he needed was for the gemsbok to stand still. This, however, was the tricky part. As soon as he tried to approach the gemsbok, he would stumble off into the bush. I say "stumble" because it was clear that this was a very sick animal. There was no spring in his step, and it was all he could do to move away from us. Each time he moved, we would follow, the farmer with his open Land Rover, and Melvin and me on foot. The time was now closer to eight o'clock, and the sun was warming the air. We were getting tired from having to march through the bush. Each time we thought we had our chance, we were disappointed because the gemsbok would once again take fright and move off, albeit slowly. Eventually, we must have tired the gemsbok, because he lay underneath a tree and allowed us to approach him. Melvin had a clear shot from about 30 meters (95 feet) and fired off the dart. Would you believe it? There was a small branch near the gemsbok's rump, and the dart stuck in the branch. I decided to retrieve the dart and slowly sneaked up to the animal. I was able to actually get close enough to retrieve the dart and back away without disturbing him. This great achievement was not due to my incredible stealth but sadly due to the fact that the animal was near death. I gave the dart back to Melvin, and since it had not discharged its drug, he reloaded it in his gun and successfully darted the gemsbok in the rump. We followed the animal as he stumbled off into the bush. There was no great challenge in keeping up with him; he was too sick to really get going, and within a short while he settled down again. There he stayed, lying on his chest under a shade tree.

Soon our patient went to sleep, and we wasted no time in examining him. Because of our inexperience with this species, one thing we neglected to do was to secure the animal's horns. They could be lethal if the gemsbok was still even slightly awake. One toss of his head, and we could have become shish kebabs. We were fortunate this didn't happen.

We began our general inspection of the gemsbok's skin and hooves. We noted a heavy tick burden, dehydration, and infected fetlock joints, as well as probably a heavy worm burden. There were wounds and scratches on his skin as well, from stumbling through thorn bushes and branches. These are all typical signs of translocation sickness. If this were a small animal, like a dog or cat, I would have given it intravenous fluids and tried to rehydrate it. Melvin elected not to do this. Instead he poured on a topical tick preparation, and we administered an injectable dewormer. I suggested that we give the gemsbok some antibiotics, and I also felt that a shot of steroids would do no harm. After all this was done, we administered the antidote to the sedative. The blood pressure of the animal was low, so it was difficult finding a vein. The antidote had to be given intravenously. Having given many a kitten an intravenous injection, I felt confident that hitting a vein in a gemsbok would be no big deal. We raised an ear vein, and I administered the antidote into this vein. Within a few minutes we could see consciousness return, but, unfortunately, our patient was so weak that he could not rise. He lay recumbent on his chest and looked much debilitated. He did not even try to rise, which was a grave sign. In hindsight, we realized that the poor animal was doomed before we even started. But where there is life, there is hope, and at the time we felt that trying to treat the gemsbok was worthwhile.

It is a cardinal rule that a veterinarian should never leave an unconscious patient in the care of a layperson. We, however, had to travel back to the university, and there were deadlines to meet. We had no choice other than to hand over the patient to the farmer. Once we were sure that our patient was awake, albeit not ambulatory, we took our leave. The gemsbok still had not risen, and this was a bad sign. Usually, animals get up within a short time of an antidote being administered. We gave the farmer instructions about caring for the patient. It was important that the animal stay in the shade, and it was also important that he should rise, eat, and drink before the day was done. We had done the best we could, and now it was up to the farmer to implement our instructions, but more importantly, it was up to nature to take its course.

The next day our gemsbok was dead.

It is always sad when a patient dies. I don't believe that any creature should die alone. Whether it is a wild animal or a domestic pet, if I can, I want to give my fellow creature comfort in its dying moments. I am not sure if it really makes a difference, but I can say anecdotally from many hundreds of times that I have done this that I think the poor departing animal knows I am there and somehow receives comfort. I was saddened by the gemsbok's dying and also saddened that he died alone. I know that many animals die alone, but I would have preferred to be present for this gemsbok's final moments of life.

Death is part of a vet's job. Sometimes we administer last rites to our departing patients, and sometimes we are actually called upon to euthanize them. Fortunately, more often than not, our patients live, and there is an ending that one can smile and feel good about.

I look back on the gemsbok with mixed emotions. I was glad to have been given the opportunity of helping but sad that we were not able to acquit ourselves better. Each experience, however, is cumulative, and the mistakes that we make act as good lessons for the future. I am fairly sure that the outcome would probably have been the same in this case. The gemsbok died not due to inadequate treatment but rather to disastrous capture techniques. Only educating owners and farmers on using suitably qualified game capturers would have made a difference here.

Chapter 10

Cheetahs on the Edge

CHEETAHS ARE ON THE EDGE OF EXTINCTION. THEIR NUMBERS IN THE wild are almost at a level that is not sustainable. If things don't change dramatically, in a few short years, these magnificent animals will be gone. All its speed and power will not save the cheetah from the challenges that have been placed before it, such as hunting, poaching, and an ever-decreasing habitat. Right now, if it was not for the reservoir of captive breeding stock, many people believe that the cheetah would be further along the road of extinction than it is already. Possibly the biggest threat to the cheetah and most other wild animals is their ever-eroding habitat. Farms are established in wilderness areas, and the wild animals have to move out to make way for domestic ones. Fortunately, this trend seems to have slowed down and in some areas has reversed. Not only do the farms take up land that was inhabited by wild animals, but also, more importantly, the traditional migration routes of prey animals such as wildebeest have been fractured. Even one farm straddling a migration route can have an impact far beyond its physical size. We have a lot of work still to do to safeguard wildlife for our children's heritage.

Kapama is a private game reserve in the Hoedspruit region. It lies along the western border of Kruger National Park. Among its many distinctions, it is the home to the Cheetah Project. This is an endeavor by one woman named Lente Roode. She has set her goals on trying to ensure that certain endangered species are at least well represented in captivity. It is her hope to have a breeding program so successful that its by-product is the ability to repopulate wild areas with cheetahs. She has been successful to the point that the project is able to sell surplus cheetahs to other game reserves, thus expanding the population. Today Kapama has the world's largest captive population of cheetahs. This in itself is a tribute to the project's success. And it is really against the odds, because cheetahs are very difficult to breed.

My friend and mentor Professor Dave Meltzer is a world authority on cheetah breeding. He has been involved in the project's breeding program for many years, and its success is in no small measure due to him. One of the challenges facing the breeding program is that the male cheetahs are all mostly subfertile, meaning that their sperm count is low, almost too low to fertilize a female. In addition to this, much of their sperm cells have abnormalities. This challenge requires regular monitoring of cheetah semen. By anesthetizing the cheetahs and then electroejaculating them, their semen is harvested. Once the semen has been harvested in this manner, it is examined microscopically and evaluated for fertility.

I was visiting Peter Rogers at the Cheetah Project and was lucky enough to be there at the same time as Professor Meltzer. To see him in action is a rare privilege. He was there to evaluate the semen of four cheetahs to see which one would make the most suitable sire for one or two of the females that were coming into season.

Peter's role was to go out and dart the cheetahs and deliver them to Professor Meltzer so that he could examine their sperm. Peter had done this many times, and without much fuss he was able to deliver two sleeping cheetahs within about a half hour. (The reason that only two at a time were brought in is because the pickup used for the transport had room for only two animals.) Each one was darted and anesthetized, then placed in a transport crate and taken to the wildlife hospital at the Cheetah Project where Professor Meltzer waited. Once there, they were unloaded and brought inside. They were still asleep when they were placed on the operating table. The method used to collect semen is a bit too similar to techniques used in a medieval torture chamber to go into in detail here. Suffice it to say that it is done with the cheetahs sound asleep, and they experience no pain or suffering at any time, ever.

Once the cheetahs' semen was collected, Professor Meltzer evaluated it using a phase contrast microscope. This provides light filtered in such a way that one can actually examine the morphology of individual sperm cells. A sperm cell should have a distinct head, a neck structure, and a tail. If there are abnormalities in the actual structure of a sperm cell, then it will be unable to fertilize an ovum. Professor Meltzer also evaluated the motility of the sperm by observing them swimming around under the microscope. If their motility is impaired, they will not be able to reach their targets. The sperm from the first cheetah that we examined was hopeless. His concentration of sperm cells was very low. The percentage of abnormal sperm cells was also far too high for fertilization to occur. Instead of swimming in a straight line, these sperm were going round in circles. The conclusion that Professor Meltzer came to after examining this cheetah's sperm was that the animal was infertile. There could be nutritional and stress factors, as well as many other ones, and if in this cheetah's future some or all of these factors changed, then it was possible for the cheetah to become fertile. For the present, however, the animal was incapable of fertilizing a female.

Professor Meltzer performed the same procedure on the next sleeping cheetah with very similar results. The second animal was also infertile. In fact, the second cheetah had produced an ejaculate with no sperm at all.

While Professor Meltzer was performing the procedures on the two sleeping cheetahs, Peter went out to the enclosures where two other males were being kept. Without much fuss, Professor Meltzer had the next two cheetahs brought to him, sleeping and ready for his not so tender ministrations.

Within an hour, all four cheetahs had been electroejaculated, and their semen had been evaluated. The results were disappointing, to say the least. One animal had semen that was of sufficient quality that he could have been used to breed with at that point in time. The other three were completely subfertile. If the survival of the species rested on these four animals, then the species was in deep trouble.

These results were not all that unusual. Professor Meltzer told us that over the many years that he had been involved in the evaluation of cheetah semen, this was the general pattern. On average only one in ten cheetahs had semen of a sufficient quality to ensure fertilization. Because of this, the various breeding institutions throughout the world had adopted a "reverse harem" setup, which provided for more than one male for each female in the breeding colony. This stacked the odds in favor of a fertile mating, because if there is more than one male, it is hoped that one of them will be fertile at the time of mating. This in itself is in direct contrast with nature. In the natural environment, the males usually assemble a harem of females around them, and in this way they successfully fertilize more than one female at a time, thus maximizing the breeding potential of their harem. The harem system, however, only works when there is a dominant fertile male. When a population of animals drops below a certain number, the hybrid vigor associated with great genetic variation is lost. The individual animals may in fact have some abnormality due to too small a gene pool. This is probably why fertility in the small population of remaining cheetahs is so low. This may in fact also be the case within the wild population, thus further exacerbating the problem and thereby reducing the chances of the cheetah surviving into the future.

At the Cheetah Project, the reverse harem setup seems to work. The females that are in season are allowed to run in camps that have males in long enclosures next to them. In this way, the females are stimulated by the presence of the males, and the males are stimulated by the presence of the females. The animals are observed, and the male that seems to be the most interested in the estrus female is allowed to try to mate with her. This has been moderately successful, and most of the females have had litters using this method. They produce litters of baby cheetahs once a year on average. The litters normally have two babies.

The success of the breeding program is measured by the number of offspring produced. This is a direct measurement. No babies, no success. It is as simple as that. The Cheetah Project can be proud of its achievements. It has the largest captive breeding population in the world today. It produces enough cheetahs so that they are able to sell excess stock off to other institutions throughout the world, and at any time that visitors go there, they may view mothers with their offspring at various stages of infanthood.

After finishing with the males, we stood next to an enclosure containing a mother with her babies. They were about three months old and had all the cuteness of young animals. Their fur was soft and fluffy. They were small, and they mewled like kittens. They still suckled from their mother at this tender age. They were helpless little infants that needed their mother for protection and sustenance. They were also a successful litter produced against all odds due to the dedication of outstanding vets such as Professor Meltzer and Dr. Rogers.

It is at times like these that I swell with pride, knowing that a member of my profession has been instrumental in ensuring that my children and possibly my grandchildren will have the opportunity to view these magnificent creatures with which we share the planet.

Chapter 11

Jabu

ON A WARM EVENING ONE EARLY AUTUMN, THE SETTING SUN SUNK LOW over the horizon in the Klasseri Reserve on the western border of Kruger National Park. This year there had been too little rain. The soil was dry and dusty, and the grasses were starting to turn yellow at their tips.

The water pans and dams were also much drier than they should have been. The approaches to the water holes are usually surrounded by hard, compact dirt from the many paws and hooves that trample the earth. There is usually just a small fringe of soft mud at the water's edge. But when the rains are scarce, and the air and the earth are dry, the mud fringe expands. As the water recedes, the muddy zone can increase dramatically in size. This year the mud zone was at its maximum.

For an animal weighing 3 tons, this presents no problem at all. In fact, the mud zone is a favorite area for elephants to wallow and coat their hard, tough hides with mud. Once the mud dries, the elephants scrape their bodies against rough trees, rubbing off the insects and parasites that stick to their skin, and giving themselves blessed relief. For a baby elephant, however, the mud zone can be a death trap.

Jabu was just three months old. He was born at the beginning of summer, usually an excellent time for calving. This year things were a little different. The rains were early and light. The plains had just enough water to provide grass and leaves for his mother to eat. She was able to provide him with the rich milk that he needed to ensure that he grew at the normal rate. Jabu was adorable, like all baby elephants are at that age. Still slightly unstable on his feet, he'd gambol next to his mother, his tiny trunk waving and ears constantly flapping to keep him cool through the long, hot summer. Jabu was born into an extended family fiercely protective of their young and willing to go to extreme lengths to protect them from danger. His mother, along with three "aunties," had left the herd briefly to give birth. The three aunties took their duties very seriously and kept guard during the birthing process. Once Jabu was born, they helped wherever they could. They fussed over him and made sure that he kept pace when they were walking. When he played, one of the attendant elephants always kept an indulgent and protective eye on him. His mother and the three aunties made a formidable team if predators were around. The four of them formed a large, impenetrable gray wall behind which he could hide in safety. Altogether, Jabu was safe and protected, and his chances of survival were good.

The four females and their small charge had not yet rejoined the main herd of about one hundred elephants. Elephant herds are highly structured and are led by a dominant matriarch. The matriarch of this herd was a wise old female who had lived through more than forty summers. She knew the area well, and her instinct made her restless—there had not been enough rain that summer, and it was time to move on in search of water. She had lived through drought before and knew what to do. There were areas where humans had drilled wells into the earth, and windmills pumped the precious water into large concrete containers. The containers were high but presented no great challenge to a 3-meter-tall (10-foot) animal with a mobile trunk that could reach another 3 meters.

The matriarch marshaled her herd and through a series of sounds too low in frequency for the human ear conveyed her message to them. Without much questioning, the herd followed her. The three aunties and Jabu's mother were not too concerned about the migration. Although Jabu would be hard-pressed to keep up with a herd that could walk comfortably at 12 kilometers (7 miles) an hour for the entire day, he would manage if his mother and aunties slowed down to accommodate him. They could easily follow the path left by the migrating herd and would catch up in time. The four females were also more than capable of defending themselves in the face of danger, and they knew where to find the wells. And so they set off, confident that in time they would see the dry months through with the rest of the herd.

To anyone lucky enough to see them, their migration was a magnificent sight. Instinct bade them to graze and rest during the day, and to drink their fill when they came across water. Dusk and dawn would find them moving silently and steadily through the bush with just the creak of a branch or the snap of a twig underfoot to signal their presence. In the late afternoon, the sun caused the dust surrounding these moving giants to glow red.

Jabu was managing the journey well so far. Still, by the end of the first week, they were about one day's march behind the main herd. Dawn on the ninth day of their journey found the five elephants marching with purpose in the direction of the rest of the herd. Soon they arrived at the edge of a water hole. It was usually filled with an abundance of fresh, clear water, but not this year. The lack of rain had left only a little muddy water, and the border of the water hole was soft, treacherous mud. The females paused, aware of the danger that the mud posed to Jabu. But it was too late. Trumpeting with delight, he ran toward the thick black sludge. His momentum took him through the edge of the water hole, but then he fell, flailing wildly, churning the mud until he had sunk down to his belly. Quiet now, and terrified, he heard the warning signals of his mother to keep still. This was a signal he knew well. It had been issued to him many times when predators were close by, and now he obeyed instantly. His mother lumbered up close to him and tried to wrap her trunk around his little head to pull him out. But as soon as she exerted pressure, he squealed in pain. Clearly, this would not work. She tried to use her trunk to push him from behind, but all this did was to drive his head into the mud. It is an anomaly that the elephant, the largest and most powerful land animal, is unable to lift its young.

By now Jabu was stuck fast, and the four females stood beside him, helpless and distressed. They sprayed him with water, and he drank from his mother, but there was nothing else they could do. Slowly and reluctantly, they realized that their baby was doomed. The small herd stayed together for the day and gave the baby shelter from the sun and kept him cool by dowsing him with water, but as the cool of the evening approached, the powerful instinct of survival came to the fore. Knowing that the young animal was destined to die, the instinct for the adults to continue along their journey became overwhelming. There was nothing more they could do for Jabu.

It is a strange and marked difference between animals and humans. Humans will sacrifice their lives in defense of their children. In the animal world, however, the adult will defend its young vigorously but not to the death. When all appears lost, the adult will give up in order to survive and procreate again. For animals, survival of the species resides in the adults, but the human view is that the future of humanity rests in its youth.

The four adults started to move off in the dusk, leaving the terrified little elephant behind. The baby lay quietly, trapped firmly in the mud, which is where he was found about twelve hours later by a ranger whose dawn patrol took him near the water hole. The ranger noticed what appeared to be the carcass of a baby elephant. Vultures were circling overhead, indicating death. The ranger had spotted them earlier and decided to have a look. The area he was responsible for was vast, about 2,500 square kilometers (965 square miles). This area of patrol was a mere speck in the vast wildlife reserve in which the elephants were migrating.

With one glance the ranger took in the tragic situation. The circling vultures had not yet settled down to feed. The large footprints in the mud and the signs of the struggle told their eloquent story. He correctly guessed that the little elephant had got stuck, and the adults had tried in vain to rescue him. He drove his game vehicle to the edge of the mud to have a closer look with his binoculars. It wouldn't be long now before the vultures would settle and feed off the carcass that remained.

Suddenly, a large eye opened and blinked feebly in the morning light. The little trunk stirred pathetically. The ranger was stunned; the baby elephant was alive. Although time was not on his side, his first thought was to try to save it. The first call he made was to his assistants to bring straps to pull the elephant out of the mud. Next, he made a call to Peter Rogers, then the resident vet at the reserve. A few words were all that was needed to mobilize the rescue team. Within a half hour the team had assembled at the muddy trap and got down to work. The baby was too weak to struggle, so when the ranger approached with the large web belts that would be tied around him, all that he could do was look fearfully at him and once again feebly wave his trunk. Straps were secured around the baby's neck, and the ranger was able to push a strap under the front legs and around the chest. The straps were then secured to the tail bar of the game vehicle. Using its power as well as gentle traction by the ranger and his helper, the team was eventually able to rescue the once doomed young elephant.

Now that Jabu was freed from the mud, Peter was able to examine him. He saw at once that the baby was badly dehydrated and in shock, and needed intravenous fluids immediately. The rangers decided that the elephant should be taken to the Cheetah Project, the endangered species center situated on the Kapama private game reserve near Hoedspruit. Here he would be hospitalized at the wildlife hospital run by Peter.

Nursing a baby elephant back to health is a full-time job. The hospital staff had to keep the little fellow company twenty-four hours a day, seven days a week. They named him Jabu, which means "happiness." He was kept on rehydration fluids intravenously for twenty-four hours, and then the drip line was removed. He seemed more stable and a little brighter. He was given a course of antibiotics to treat his skin, which had become infected from being immersed in the mud for so long, and was also treated for shock. He had to be taught how to suckle from a bottle because he was not yet eating solids.

The next few days were crucial in determining whether Jabu would live or die. The hospital staff pulled out all the stops to give him the best chance of survival. Luckily, he was small enough to be handled, and he became calmer as he got to know the nurses at the hospital.

There is a fine line between life and death in animals like Jabu after they have been through an ordeal like this. But sometime on the third day of his treatment at the hospital, he crossed that line over to the safe side. His spirits rose, his appetite increased, and it seemed as though he would in fact survive, much to the joy of all the hospital staff. His treatment was not complete, and he would still have to stay in the hospital for another ten days or so, but it was time to actually start making plans for his future. He and his species live a long time, sometimes up to sixty or seventy years. They also grow up to be very large (a fully grown bull elephant can weigh over 6 tons), so choosing a home for him was an important consideration. Everyone involved agreed that he should not have a temporary home; a permanent solution was needed.

Lente Roode of the Cheetah Project was approached and asked if Jabu could make his home in Kapama, initially as part of the Cheetah Project and ultimately possibly as one of the elephants that would carry people around the reserve. She agreed to the proposal, and this is how Jabu became part of the Cheetah Project. But baby elephants need company to survive and thrive. The herd usually forms this vital element of the baby's upbringing. From a very early age, the adults instill discipline into young elephants. There are do's and don'ts that are enforced by the herd. Without this discipline, many orphan elephants raised in captivity by humans grow up to be juvenile delinquents with deviant behavior, as we had seen with Temba. Bearing this in mind, the team at Kapama set about trying to enforce certain rules of behavior that would, if not prevent delinquency, at least mitigate against the worst vices that captive-reared elephants acquire.

The first matter to attend to was the appointment of a permanent handler who would bond with Jabu. A permanent handler must accept his or her responsibility but also has to be accepted by the baby. It is no use trying to foist an inappropriate person on a baby elephant. The match is very important for future behavior. One or two people at the Cheetah Project volunteered, but within a few days it was seen that they were unsuitable.

Flippie Botha was a student employed at the Cheetah Project during his holidays. He was approaching the end of his course on wildlife management, and the little elephant seemed to have a strong affinity for him. Whenever Flippie passed near little Jabu, he became very excited. Flippie is a soft-spoken, gentle person who at the same time is physically very strong. Whenever he had the chance, he would pass by the elephant enclosure and always had time to stroke and talk to Jabu. Clearly, this was a very good match, and after some discussion at management level, it was decided to offer

Flippie the post of caretaker for Jabu. Flippie was about to take his final examinations, and, if all went well, he could be available for duty within a month. He could then take up his post as Jabu's keeper. Flippie jumped at the opportunity, and shortly after passing his finals, he took up a permanent post as Jabu's caretaker at Kapama.

Jabu's routine was established. He was still bottle-fed and had quickly learned how to suckle from the large bottle that was used to feed him. He was fed every four hours with a milk supplement specially designed for the needs of a rapidly growing elephant. The bottle-feeding would be his sole source of nutrition until he was about six months old, at which point some solids would be introduced into his diet. This would be considered early in the wild, but in a human-reared situation, it is acceptable. Thankfully, the task of rearing a baby elephant was not virgin territory, and the staff at the Cheetah Project had many cases of hand-reared elephants to refer to.

Jabu thrived and grew. His relationship with Flippie flourished. The bond between them now is a beautiful thing to see, and it was established by Flippie's commitment to the little elephant. For the first year of the relationship, Flippie slept in Jabu's enclosure. During the cold winter months, they slept in a stable, and in the warm summer months, they often slept under the stars. When Jabu was considered old enough, Flippie started to leave the little elephant alone for certain times during the day. This weaning process is similar to that which happens in the wild. At about one year of age, baby elephants start to venture a few hundred meters from the main herd and try to graze by themselves. This also allowed Flippie some time off. Every morning and every evening, come rain or shine, Flippie and Jabu went for a walk along the perimeter fence. The walk would sometimes take as long as an hour. This was an important part of the socialization process and allowed Jabu to see the world.

The day that I first met Jabu, he and Flippie were returning from their evening walk. Jabu was then two years old. He stood almost as tall as I am. His shoulder was just shorter than mine. He still had all the cuteness of a baby elephant, but he weighed in at an impressive 600 kilograms (1,320 pounds). His behavior was exemplary for an orphan elephant. He had been taught not to rush at people and to be gentle with them. Like all baby elephants, he loved to play, and his playfulness with the water hose was especially endearing. He seemed to know that he was up to mischief, but that this small indulgence was permitted. Flippie proudly showed off his scars and broken bones, which were mute testimony to the power of even so young an elephant. The scary thought was that Jabu was still going to grow to at least six times his present size.

I have had the great pleasure of observing this little elephant grow over the last few years of my visits to the area. Because I am not there constantly, I am able to appreciate how much he has grown. He was six years old at the time of this writing, and he is now fully grown and probably weighs more than 4,000 kilograms (8,800 pounds), which is over 4 metric tons. He is not yet a delinquent, and we all hope that he will not be one.

Jabu is a very important feature of life at Kapama. He is a part of the elephant back safari venture there and is successfully integrated into the program. His story is at once heartbreaking and heart-warming. He is testimony to the commitment of dedicated people who make Africa and its animals their life's work.

Chapter 12

Manwane

THE WORD GAME HAS A NUMBER OF DIFFERENT MEANINGS. IN THE context of these stories, *game* refers to the wild animals that roam the plains of Africa. If one talks about sports, then *game* refers to the playing of the sport. Playing the game can also mean cooperating with someone or something. Being game to do something implies being willing or cooperative. The game ranger is all of the above and so much more. He is the marshal and custodian of the wildlife on our continent. He is a player of sport with such physical dedication that he is able to hike the plains of Africa with ease, often walking marathon distances daily in his patrols. He is willing to go not just the extra mile, but also the extra hundred miles. He is also a very "game" ranger, prepared to do whatever it takes to get the job done and secure the outcome. These wonderful individuals are indispensable in the wildlife world. They are its unsung heroes.

This is a story about a game ranger whose name I do not even know, but for the sake of the story, I'll call him Adam. I heard it from one of my colleagues who took part in the adventure.

It was almost the end of a hot and dusty day toward the end of summer. The sun was large and red and low on the horizon. Adam had been out since before dawn and was looking forward to getting back to his modest home. He had thought about what he would eat that evening and had decided to treat himself to a mug of coffee, possibly laced with brandy and sweetened with some honey. He would enjoy a quiet hour on his porch, listening to the sounds of Africa, and then blissful slumber. He was driving his patrol vehicle, an open Land Rover, and was about a half hour away from getting back. There was a small kopje about 100 meters (110 yards) ahead, and he decided to stop there, switch off his engine, and just observe the bush and its sounds for a few minutes before heading home.

He sat there savoring the sounds of Africa at dusk. The grazers would still feed a bit before settling down for the night, the daytime animals would be heading for their holes and lairs, and the nocturnal animals would be getting ready for their business of the night. The panoramic cycle of life that has repeated itself for countless years would do so yet once more tonight.

His ears were sharp, having listened to the sounds of the bush for many years. He spent a lot of time in solitude, and this also honed his instincts.

The hair on his arms and at the nape of his neck suddenly stood on end. Something was wrong. He listened carefully for the noise that must have registered first in his subconscious.

There it was. It sounded like hyenas making a kill. But there was something else, a squealing that he could not identify. Hyenas prey on anything they can but usually end up eating carrion. The sounds were coming from the east. That was to his right as he sat in his car. Something was wrong. He quickly started the Land Rover and headed for them, all thoughts of home forgotten.

He guessed that the sounds were ½ kilometer (⅓ mile) away. That would take him about five or six minutes of negotiating the bush at dusk. He switched his lights on and gripped the steering wheel to control his vehicle. As he got closer, it became easier to locate the actual spot because the sounds increased in volume. They were coming from just ahead, behind a thicket. He swung the vehicle around, expecting the hyenas to disperse, but as his headlights illuminated the ground, he saw that his instincts had been correct.

There were six hyenas surrounding a baby rhino that could not have been more than five or six months old; they were charging the baby and nipping its flanks and limbs. In turn, it was defending itself with a ferocity beyond its tender age. A six-month-old baby rhino can weigh up to 300 kilograms (660 pounds) and can still present itself as a formidable foe. One butt from its head with its little horn bud can fracture ribs and break limbs. Even though it was outnumbered and outgunned, it was no pushover, and the hyenas were taking no chances. Until Adam's arrival, the end would have been inevitable, but now things were different.

Adam drove straight for the hyenas and honked the horn. He hoped this would scare them off and give him a chance to try to save the little animal. The hyenas, however, were not easily deterred from their intended meal and only backed off a few meters. The little rhino stood its ground and did not run from the vehicle. It turned around, and Adam was able to get a glimpse of its other flank. There seemed to be a large piece of intestine hanging out of a gaping wound. Something strange had happened here. Where was the mother? Adam positioned his vehicle between the hyenas and the baby rhino and kept the engine running. By revving it and honking and flashing his lights, he was able to keep the blood-hungry hyenas at bay. Thoughts of his own safety never crossed his mind. Six hyenas could easily have made a meal of a game ranger. They are not man-eaters, but given the opportunity, who knows for sure.

Multitasking comes naturally to a game ranger, and now Adam had to put that skill to use. While revving the motor and flashing the vehicle's lights, he switched on his radio and called into base. He described the situation and asked for help. The vet would also be needed, because it looked like an emergency operation was required. All this time the little rhino stood its ground, still making the squealing sounds that Adam first heard and thought out of place. The little fellow was also game in his own way and kept on mock charging the pack of hyenas that stood just outside the beams of light made by the vehicle's headlights.

Help was about an hour away, and Adam established a routine of sorts to keep the situation under control. The motor was kept running, and the lights were flashed regularly. He kept the vehicle between the rhino and the hyenas. A stalemate developed. The hyenas kept a short distance away, and the baby rhino, somehow realizing that Adam and the Land Rover represented some sort of safety, kept his distance but made sure that he was on the far side of the vehicle. Even at this tender age, he sensed that he should keep the vehicle between himself and the pack of hungry hyenas.

And this is how they were found an hour later. Two other game vehicles arrived with rangers and trackers and Peter Rogers. They all climbed out and looked at the scene in amazement. "Why did you not use your rifle, Adam?" one of the other rangers asked. "Because the hyenas are alive, and they have a right to their lives as well," was Adam's reply. "I also thought that if I fired, I might scare the baby away, and then all would have been lost. I doubt that I would have been able to find and save the little guy in the dark. As it is, I think I was just in the nick of time."

While this short conversation was going on, Peter had estimated the rhino's weight and assembled the dart he was going to use to immobilize the baby. He quietly took aim and shot the rhino in the rump. Six minutes later, the baby was sleeping, and they had the chance to examine him and see the extent of the problem. There was a gaping hole in his flank and a deep puncture wound into his abdomen. From this wound a loop of intestine hung and had been dragged in the dirt. Peter set up a drip because the little creature was showing signs of dehydration. The staff then moved the baby onto a clean tarpaulin that would have to serve as an operating table. Peter prepared his instruments and drugs and took out a container of water to scrub his hands and the wound. Using the water and a sterilizing fluid called Hibiscrub, he set about his task.

The hole really looked like a gore wound from another rhino horn. It was possible that a male rhino had tried to mate with this baby's mother and in the process had gored the baby. Where was the mother, though? The injured baby could have taken fright and ran, and the male may have herded the female away. As with so many other animals injured in the bush, we would never know exactly what had happened.

By this time the drip had been running for a few minutes, and the wound had been cleaned and sterilized. It was now time to replace the loop of intestine and suture the hole closed. This required Peter to take the loop in a gloved hand and stuff it back through the hole in the animal's flank. He used water and sterilizing fluids to lubricate the loop of intestine, and, while passing the loop back into the abdomen, he checked along its length for necrosis and puncture wounds. Amazingly, despite the loop actually having dragged along the ground, it was remarkably undamaged, just dusty and a bit dry. Once the loop was back inside, Peter was able to attend to the actual gore wound. He used a thick piece of suture material called PDS (polydioxanone) to close up the internal layers of the abdomen, then used the same material to close up the skin. Even though this was a baby, it was a pachyderm. Pachyderms have thick skins, and suturing their skin closed requires some effort.

This was done quickly and efficiently, and all that was now left to do was to bandage the wound, administer antibiotics and drugs for shock, and remove the baby to safety. It had been decided to take the baby rhino to Peter's wildlife hospital at Kapama and nurse him back to health there. He would require antibiotics and careful monitoring postop to maximize his chances of survival.

The hyenas had given up their quest once the reinforcements had arrived, so now all that was required was to load the 300-kilogram (660-pound) sleeping baby onto the back of one of the game vehicles and drive him to the hospital. This required the efforts of all the people that were there that night: two strong game rangers, two trackers, and a vet. Once the baby was safely loaded, the journey back to the wildlife hospital started. This was not far as the crow flies, but it was now pitch dark, and the vehicles were off what little tracks there were. Adam took the lead and acted as a path blazer. His driving ability through the bush was excellent. He chose the easiest routes that would also do the least damage to the bush. The drive took a half hour. They arrived at the hospital, and all hands were required to once again manhandle the baby out of the transport vehicle. By this time he was waking up. He was placed in a small enclosure that doubled as a hospital cage for small to medium-size herbivores. Peter decided to administer the antidote to the sedative, and within a very short time of this injection, the little rhino fully woke up. He took some tottering steps in his new enclosure. The evening was warm, and it was felt that he would be safe enough here. He would still require regular feeding, and a large bottle with a teat was prepared, as he was still suckling. The nursing staff was roped in, and a routine was set up. A milk formula was mixed and tested on the little guy, and he seemed quite happy to drink it.

It took two weeks before the bandages were removed, and to everyone's delight, the wound had closed up uneventfully. Lente Roode allowed the little rhino to live in one of the camps at the Cheetah Project, and there he stayed for two years.

I met him when he had been there for about nine months, and he must have weighed 600 kilograms (1,320 pounds) by then. Another rescued rhino named Dave, in honor of Professor Dave Meltzer, accompanied him. The two of them made a great pair. They were not exactly tame, but they were used to humans to the point that if you approached them slowly and carefully and talked all the while to them, they would allow you to stroke them. This is a rare experience. They are amazingly primitive to look at, and their skin, while being very thick, is also very sensitive. They actually seem to enjoy being scratched. Their heads are massive and can pivot amazingly. Their necks are very short, and the power that is generated by this fulcrum is awesome. If they toss their heads and you are in the way, you will be seriously injured, if not by their horn, then just by the sheer power generated by this movement. It was a great joy to stand alongside the fence and call them to me by name. Their sight is poor and their memory bad, so if you don't talk to them all the time, they tend to forget you are there.

Adam came to see his rescued rhino on a regular basis, and in fact was instrumental in naming him Munwane, which is the name of a small river running close to where Adam found him. The relationship between the two of them was special. I don't know if Munwane had any knowledge that Adam had rescued him, but the interaction between the two of them was different. Munwane became gentle and would almost nuzzle Adam with what looked like affection.

At the end of the two-year period, it was decided to allow the two rhinos to join the main herd at Kapama. They lived there for a few months, and then tragically Munwane was found dead. A poacher had killed him. His small horn had been cruelly hacked from his head and was probably sold to a muti shop for a paltry sum.

What price a life?

Adam was devastated by the news. He felt that he should never have intervened. Had the hyenas killed the rhino originally, then at least some sort of natural cycle would have occurred.

I don't know what the answers are; all I know is that the rescued rhino gave many people pleasure, and everyone who came in contact with him and Dave came away just a little more sensitized to these marvelous animals. Maybe that was the purpose intended for Munwane.

CHAPTER 13

A Noose around the Neck

POACHING IS A PROBLEM THAT IS ENDEMIC TO GAME RESERVES AND wilderness areas throughout the world. The top people in the poaching world are wealthy, but their foot soldiers are poverty stricken, and when they can earn a meal ticket by killing off game animals for their masters, they do so without a second thought for the innocent animals that succumb to their dirty business. Their methods are for the most part cruel and uncaring. They range from gin traps to landmines to blasting animals with AK-47 automatic rifles. The end is to destroy the animal and take from it that which the poaching lords consider valuable. In the case of elephants, it is their tusks; rhinos, their horns; and lions, leopards, and cheetahs, their skins. Some poor animals are accidentally trapped and die because they stumbled into a trap not even meant for them.

There is also now a thriving demand for what has become known as "bush meat." This is the flesh from all animals without regard for species, scarcity, or whether they are herbivorous or carnivorous. If an animal can be killed and butchered and rendered acceptable for the pot, it is called bush meat. It is quite inconceivable that the most rare mountain gorillas, bordering on extinction and also known as man's closest relative, end up as bush meat to feed a hungry belly.

The poacher's traps are very indiscriminate. There are some methods, however, that really defy imagination when it comes to cruelty. I believe that one of the worst is the wire noose. This simple device is made with wire freely obtainable from a hardware store. I have even seen wire coat hangers bent to form a wire noose trap. They are set in the bush and are absolutely indiscriminate in what animals they snare. Once the hapless animal is snared, only then does the suffering begin. The poacher will monitor his traps only once or twice a week. An animal caught in a trap may be held captive for three to five days before the poacher returns. In that time, it may sever its leg as a result of its struggle. In the case of a predator, the animal may actually gnaw off its own leg. The poor creature usually dies of thirst and hunger before the poacher returns to dispatch it. In many cases the animal caught in a snare becomes easy prey for another predator. On very rare occasions, the snare breaks off, leaving an ever-tightening wire noose around the animal's neck or limb. If this does not kill the animal by choking it, then the wire noose cuts deeply into the flesh. Death due to infection usually occurs, and this may take days to weeks. The cost in suffering is enormous; the gain to the poacher is minimal. Often the poacher will find only the broken body of his prey with the skins damaged to the extent that they are useless. Or sometimes it is a broken trap, with the animal having escaped with the ever-tightening noose around its neck. It will die somewhere in the bush, and the poacher will go home empty-handed.

Combating the scourge known as poaching must occur at many levels. One cannot just hunt poachers. One has to also attack the markets they serve by making the objects that are manufactured from the poached animals undesirable. Making a legal supply of ivory available from large stockpiled supplies of tusks needs to be considered. This may reduce the demand for ivory, and while only a temporary solution, it seems to me to be more acceptable than burning these vast piles of tusks from animals whose lives have been sacrificed. In the case of rhino horns, education to try to dispel the myths of the horns' magical and herbal properties may lessen demand. A concerted effort to unmask and control the poachers' masters must also be made. The task is multifactorial and vast, and it is unlikely that it will be solved for a long time. All that can be done for the present is to try to control poaching at the level of the poacher by using regular antipoaching patrols implemented by dedicated personnel wherever there is wildlife. The remaining tasks need political will to be effective. Without it there can be no attacking the head of the problem. There is an old axiom: Cut off the head, and the body will die. Remove the poaching lords from their position, and the lowly foot soldiers, the actual poachers, will have no paymasters and will possibly cease their activity.

There is a game reserve just outside the small bush-veld town of Hoedspruit, the center of the game industry in South Africa. The reserve's name is Mhlametsi. The head ranger's name is Guy Arkel. On one of his patrols through the reserve, Guy noticed that one of the lionesses had a wound on her neck. On careful examination with a pair of binoculars, he saw that the lioness had a poacher's noose around her neck and a vicious wound forming from it. This was a job for a vet, so Peter Rogers was called in. The plan was to dart the lioness, remove the noose, and clean and repair the wound.

On the designated day, Peter came in and did what they had planned. The lioness was anesthetized, and the snare was removed from around her neck. The wound was bad, and it was impossible to do much surgically except to clean it and debride it. This involved cutting away dead tissue and applying antibiotic ointments to the wound, as well as inject-ing antibiotics and anti-inflammatory drugs into the sleeping lioness. Once this was done, she was allowed to wake up, and Guy was told that he needed to monitor her progress to ensure that the wound healed properly.

Usually such wounds heal uneventfully, provided the noose is removed in time, but with this lioness, it was noticed over the next few months that whenever she drank water, a patch of wetness seemed to leak out from the old wound. It was also noticed that when she ate, small pieces of food would fall out from a hole in her neck.

Peter was called in once again, and on careful examination with binoculars, he determined that an esophageal fistula had formed. This is a specific condition where a hole develops between the food pipe, or esophagus, and the outer wall of muscle and skin. Whenever the lioness ate or drank and swallowed, a small amount of food or water would leak through the hole. The lioness was observed for another few weeks because it was hoped that the fistula would close up on its own, but after nearly a month of observation, it was decided that surgery was the only option.

I must digress here for a moment to expound on two philosophies that exist within the wildlife world. There are those people who believe that nature must take its course, and the animal must live or die without human intervention. Then there are those of us who believe that the situation that animals find themselves in is already so artificial that intervention is a logical conclusion to the massive intervention already inflicted by humans. There are very few natural wilderness areas. All the game reserves are artificial, and migratory routes have been severed. Many small private game reserves have purchased their stock at great expense, and it is in their financial interest to attend to sick animals properly. In the case of this lioness, poachers caused the wound. If humans inflict the wound or are witness to it in some way, I see no reason why they can't repair it. I once saw a wildlife film about a pride of lions that had hunted and killed a zebra. In the process, a lioness was kicked, and her jaw was broken.

She was rendered incapable of hunting and was unable to drink. The film crew continued to film her and documented her death over a week. I fail to see the entertainment or educational value of this piece of footage. Why was a vet not called in to dispatch the animal in a humane way?

In case you're still wondering, I believe it is our duty to attend to animals' injuries to the best of our ability. We have eroded their habitat and created artificial areas for our fellow creatures, and I believe that it is our absolute and unquestionable obligation to look after them. And if the best of our ability involves surgical intervention, then so be it. It is the least we can do. To stand by and watch an animal die in the name of conservation is inhumane and contrary to the spirit in which we merrily enclose them in artificial areas whose borders we impose. There, now I have that off my chest, and we can get on with the story.

The lioness's esophageal fistula needed repair. This could only be done under general anesthesia, so on a designated date, we decided to find the lioness and dart her and surgically repair the problem. I flew in from Cape Town, and after a restful night in the tented camp at Kapama, we met Peter at the Mhlametsi game reserve early the next morning. Guy and his assistant game ranger met us at the lodge. They had instructed trackers to go into the bush to try to locate the lioness early that morning. So far they had found the spoor but had not yet sighted the lioness. We all climbed aboard the reserve's game vehicle and started off into the bush to try to meet up with the trackers. We were in radio contact with them, and they told us that they were onto the spoor.

The vehicle took us to within a few hundred meters of where the trackers were, and from there we had to go the rest of the way on foot because the bush was too dense to drive through. We started off through the bush in single file, led by Guy with his rifle at the ready. I followed next, then came the rest of the small group. Within a few moments, we were with the two trackers. Guy spoke to them and came back and told us that they were onto fresh spoor and felt that the lioness was not far ahead. With a measure of fear, I followed Guy and the trackers. I kept thinking that this was not exactly safe. This was dense bush, and it was entirely possible that we would stumble onto the lioness. We were in her territory, and the element of danger was physically palpable. The trackers kept looking at the ground and pointing. I tried to see what they were looking at but saw nothing. I began to start doubting them. They could just be leading us on a merry chase through the bush with no lions anywhere nearby. I actually started to relax as this thought took hold of me. Silly me.

We were in a small clearing with the trackers about 10 meters (11 yards) ahead of me when all hell broke loose. The trackers had stumbled onto not one but three lionesses, and they had cubs. Animals will usually run from humans, but a lioness with cubs will not. She will attack if she feels threatened, and these three females with their cubs felt very threatened, what with all these people suddenly in their faces. They roared and snarled very loudly. It is impossible to do justice to the amount of noise they generated. There were waves of sound washing over us in deep bass tones. The sound actually reverberated in our chests. I was terrified.

Guy had briefed us at the start of our hike through the bush. He had told us that if there was a problem, and one of the lionesses charged us, we were to remain absolutely motionless. Lionesses would only chase and attack a moving target. If we stood still, this would confuse them, and they would hesitate to attack. Well, difficult as it was, I stood my ground while the animals charged the trackers. Unbelievably, they too stood their ground. Guy quietly cocked his rifle and held it at the ready. This did not overly reassure me. At best, he would have enough time for one shot. There were three lionesses, and they were enraged; if they did attack us, we were in deep trouble. Once again I wished for the safety of my house overlooking the ocean in suburbia. What was I actually doing here? My heart was racing, and I really feared for my life. I stood there petrified, shivering and sweating in fear.

The standoff must have lasted about three minutes. I believe that witnessing the trackers standing completely still with an enraged pride of lionesses mock charging them was the bravest thing I have ever seen. I have no idea what steel ran through these men's veins, but I was highly impressed by their bravery. Then, as suddenly as it started, it ended. The lionesses melted back into the bush, and their young ones followed. After the noise of their attack, the silence was deafening.

After what seemed like an eternity, the trackers started to move cautiously again and gingerly backed away from where the lionesses had been. Once we were sure that they had in fact gone, we relaxed, and the trackers started to laugh with the release of tension. We were all very shaky, and Guy decided that we should head back to the safety of the game vehicle. Walking around here was not for the fainthearted, and right now my heart felt very faint.

Once back in the vehicle, we assessed the situation. The injured female we were looking for was part of this trio of lionesses. It was felt that they had been very spooked, and to try to work with them again today would not be a good idea. We had scheduled a few days in the bush to try to help the lioness, so we felt that we could wait until the next day to dart her and fix her.

Guy decided on an alternative approach. It was time to bait the lioness into coming to us. The bait, however, had to be obtained. Guy had seen a wildebeest in the bush that was sick and very thin. He noticed that one leg was badly injured, and its chances of survival were poor. He felt that it would be humane to dispatch it quickly with a bullet. This would be the bait. The gutted carcass would emit a smell that was guaranteed to attract all predators in the area.

Once the task was done, the carcass was brought to a tree in an area inhabited by the lioness we wanted. The carcass was gutted and then strung up in a tree using steel cables to a height of about 3 meters (10 feet). This was done very securely because we wanted the lioness to feed off the carcass at the site we chose. Guy told me that it was possible for an adult lion to pull the carcass down from the tree if it was not properly secured. The lion would then drag the carcass through the bush and take it far away before feeding. It is quite an awesome sight to see a male adult lion weighing about 300 kilograms (660 pounds) dragging the carcass of an animal that weighs 200 kilograms (440 pounds) through the bush for a number of kilometers. Their strength is truly impressive. The only thing preventing this was to tie the carcass up very well using steel cables.

By the time we had finished setting the bait for the lioness, it was midafternoon. We were hot and sweaty and had really been very frightened by our encounter. The aftereffects of the adrenaline release had made us tired, and we decided to go back to our tents to rest for the afternoon. We left the baited tree with a tracker sitting safely in a game vehicle. He would remain in radio contact with Guy, who would in turn call us if the lioness started feeding. We had done all we could do, and it was now time for a strategic withdrawal.

Back at the camp, we made a fire and boiled some water for coffee, then added condensed milk to our brew. This is a very evocative taste for me. It reminds me of my early days at a game reserve, when I was taken there by my parents. It also reminds me of meals on trains traveling through the

Karoo, a large desertlike expanse situated on the high inland plateau of South Africa. Besides being delicious, it is always a comforting taste and was just the thing to drink after the excitement of the morning. We took the opportunity to rest and clean up, then lay in the shade of our tents for most of the afternoon. We emerged late in the afternoon and started to discuss dinner. We were going to go to the restaurant that is situated at the old Hoedspruit railway station. We had booked to eat there that night and were looking forward to a relaxing evening.

It was just dusk when Guy called. He told us that the tracker who was observing the carcass had called in and reported that lions were close by, and that there was every possibility that our injured lioness would approach the carcass and start to feed. He had called Peter Rogers, who said that he would be available to come over, and also said that operating at night was in fact a good idea. The vehicles have bright spotlights that are used to view game at night. These would make excellent operating lights. Nighttime surgery has many advantages. It was autumn, and the nights were cool but not too cold. Once the surgery was finished, we could place the lioness in a recovery crate for the night and let her out the next morning. This would safeguard her during the recovery period.

Our supper would have to wait. We quickly dressed for the occasion once more and drove back to Mhlametsi in the hope of finding the lioness we wanted. We met Guy at the lodge once again and transferred to the game vehicle for the drive to the bait tree. We arrived there after dark and switched off the engine and waited. We could clearly hear lions communicating with each other in their low, throaty growls and grunts, and they were close to the carcass. We knew that they could smell the carcass, because so could we. We had spotlights that were powered by the car battery. The only drawback to working at night would be if the darted lioness took fright and ran into the bush. Peter, however, was confident that once she was feeding solidly, the dart would not disturb her. He had done this before, and we were relying on him for advice.

We sat for an hour or so, then a large male lion emerged from the bush and went up to the bait and sniffed. He stood on his hind legs and attempted to wrestle the carcass to the ground in order to feed. The fact that the bait was dangling from the tree slowed him down, and he was able to obtain only a small piece of meat. We also did not want him to feed too long because the lioness would not approach the carcass while the male was there. There is a hierarchy within the pride. Males feed first, and only when they have finished will the females approach the kill. We did not, however, want to frighten him off, as that might also frighten off our lioness, who we were sure was watching. It was a delicate balance.

After allowing him to feed for a quarter of an hour or so, we started the engine. The sound must have startled the lion a little, because he stood up and walked off nonchalantly. We were pleased that he had left and also satisfied that he was not too frightened. We were fairly sure that we had not startled the female away if she was there.

Unfortunately, for the next hour or so, nothing further happened. We waited and watched and got hungrier by the minute. The growling of our stomachs sounded almost as loud as the lions. Then, the real lion sounds started to fade. They were walking away and probably would not feed that night. Guy and Peter discussed the chances of success, and between the two of them it was decided that we should stand down for the night. We drove back to the lodge, then drove to the restaurant and had a belated supper.

It had been quite a day: hunting through the bush, being charged by lions, then a night adventure watching a large male lion feeding. The only thing missing was our injured female, who still needed her surgery. After a light meal, we decided to turn in. It was later than usual, and we hoped that the start of the next day would not be too early.

The next morning we awoke early but refreshed. We called Guy to ask him if the lioness had been found. Guy told us that the trackers had gone out before dawn to try to locate her. They had found the spoor but were worried because the lioness was on the move and seemed to be heading for the game fence that separates reserves from each other. The direction they were heading was east. If they managed to get over the fence, then Kruger National Park was in this direction.

This was unusual. The lioness usually hunted and rested near a water hole close to the lodge. She did not usually walk extended distances. Guy felt that the incident with the cubs and the trackers and the pride charging us must have upset them, and they were now moving to seek territory that was safer for them and their cubs.

A game fence has many different designs and many different functions. It can be used for a whole range of purposes, from keeping jackals out of a sheep enclosure, to keeping elephants in an area. It is not, however, all that good at keeping lions in one place. Like their domestic counterparts, lions can jump a fence many times their height with relative ease. They can also easily dig under a fence. Some fences have a concrete foundation, but not the one surrounding Mhlametsi. The lioness was heading for the border with intent. Guy was really worried and had asked the assistant game ranger to try to head off the lionesses if they were trying to leave the reserve. I am not sure just how effective this would be. If the animals wanted to leave, no amount of shouting and trying to head them off would help. They would simply find a time when they were undisturbed and jump the fence. If they were sufficiently frightened, they would even abandon their young in order to secure their own future. If the adults survived, they would be able to breed again. The cubs were dispensable if the species' survival was threatened. Observing this behavior again in wild animals reaffirmed to me the differences between humans and animals at this level. The baby elephant, Jabu, had been deserted by his mother when all hope seemed lost. If the survival of the lionesses was at stake, they would desert their cubs.

Guy spent a worried day in search of the animals. At times it was determined that they really were close to the trackers, but they managed to remain steadfastly out of sight. At dusk, the tired trackers returned, and a worried Guy had a very restless night. We had set aside five days to try to help with this case and were prepared to stay in the bush until the situation was resolved one way or another. We had hoped that we would still be able to complete the surgery and help the lioness. But we never did see her again.

The trackers found the place where they went over and under the fence. The adults must have dug a small channel for the cubs to get through, then jumped the fence themselves. They were headed east for the vast expanse of Kruger National Park and what they perceived to be safety.

There is a fact about Kruger that needs to be mentioned here. If you take all the area of the park that humans have access to and combine it, it amounts to less than 5 percent of the park's landmass. This consists of all the rest camps and a perimeter 100 meters (110 yards) around the outside of the camps, plus all the paths and roads and fire breaks, plus a border 10 meters (11 yards) wide on either side of the roads. Animals have over 95 percent of the park to roam about undisturbed. The lioness and her pride could literally vanish into anonymity if they reached the park.

The trackers tried to track the lioness across the adjacent reserve and found that she had once again jumped the eastern fence and was closer to the park than ever. At this point, the search was abandoned. The trackers did not have permission to track animals across the reserve that was now the lionesses' home. There was no choice but to give up. Guy reported the incident to the various lodges and game rangers who lived in the area in hopes of being able to at least monitor the lionesses' fate, but to all intents and purposes, the lions were lost to Mhlametsi.

A month or so after these dramatic events, there were reports from the rangers at Kruger that a small group of lions had arrived from a westerly direction, but they were very skittish and ran away at any human approach. Once a ranger was able to get close enough to observe that one of the female adults had quite a scar around her neck. These reports were anecdotal and unconfirmed. I like to think that they did in fact reach the relative safety and vastness of the park. Somehow this migration along routes directed by ancestral memory appeals to the romantic in me. We were unsuccessful in trying to help her surgically, but Nature showed us that she could still take care of her own.

CHAPTER 14

Crossing the Line

THE LONGER I LIVE AND WORK AS A VET, THE MORE I HAVE COME TO realize that all creatures have a right to life, and that I should do everything in my power to save them. Most of us would agree emphatically when it comes to the dogs, cats, and other animals who share our homes. But does the same ethic—this notion that all creatures have a right to life—apply to scaly, poisonous ones we instinctively want to kill? This is a question I face when the domestic world collides with the wild fringes of South Africa. When someone's pet dog bites a wild snake, and the snake then bites the dog, only sadness prevails. This story has a sad start, a sad middle, and an even sadder ending. I hope something can be learned from it, and that's why I tell it.

On the particular day that this story happened, my friend and Cape Town's "snake man," Braam Malherbe, was called out to the northern suburbs of Cape Town. There is a green swath there where people walk their dogs. The dogs are usually let off leash by their owners even though there are snakes in the area. Some of these snakes are very shy and will retreat quickly when a dog gets near. This is a good thing, because some of these snakes are also highly poisonous and do not take kindly to barking dogs. Owners should always have leashes handy, and if a dog appears to be barking frantically at something in the bush, they would be well advised to call the dog to heel and put on the leash. Unfortunately, the owner of the Staffordshire bull terrier who was one of the tragic players in this story did not have a leash handy that day. Despite being called many times, the dog continued to mock charge something in the bush. Suddenly, there was a frantic growling and snarling, and the dog rushed into a small thicket and attacked something there. Then with a yelp, it jumped back and appeared to be in great pain. Cautiously, the owner approached the bush and saw a snake coiled up there. The dog had attacked and bitten the snake, and in self-defense, the snake had bitten the dog back. If only the owner had acted more rapidly. But this was now an empty wish. The owner was able to recognize the snake and identify it as a Cape cobra. These are particularly deadly snakes, and this one was a full-grown adult about 1½ meters (5 feet) long. They bite their prey and inject their lethal venom into their victim using small, very sharp teeth, as opposed to the Egyptian cobra, which spits venom at its prey. They are also shy and nonaggressive, seeking to flee from danger as opposed to confronting it. When they do bite, they inject a neurotoxin that paralyzes respiration quickly and induces heart failure. Within a short time, the dog was in deep distress, and despite being rushed to the vet, it died.

The first instinct a person has after having his dog attacked by a snake is to try to kill the snake. This owner, however, was different. Possibly he accepted some culpability in the matter, in that he did not have a leash handy. Possibly he also realized that had he called his dog away more firmly, the dog might have listened to him. Instead of trying to kill the snake, which would also have been a dangerous thing to attempt to do, he called Braam.

Braam drove out to the area and learned that the dog was dead. The strange thing was that the snake still lay where it was found. It had not tried to move. This in itself was strange behavior. As I said before, snakes are shy animals and will flee from confrontation if possible. Braam used long tongs to fish out the snake safely. After trapping its neck, he was able to restrain the snake with his hand and examine it. There was a bite wound about ½ meter (1½ feet) from the snake's head, and because of it, the snake appeared paralyzed. The dog had bitten the snake and caused damage, but Braam was not sure just how much.

I had treated quite a number of pro bono cases for Braam. The patients were very interesting and included numerous snakes, guinea fowl, iguanas, small mammals, rodents, and birds. I did it out of personal interest and was never disappointed. He called to advise me that he was bringing the snake to my practice for me to examine and treat if possible. He placed the snake in a bag and tied the top firmly shut, and accompanied by this dangerous cargo, he rushed to my practice.

He arrived late in the afternoon and carried the bag into my prep room. It was here, at the heart of the practice, that most of the hospital work was done. Braam carefully emptied the sack onto the floor, and the adult cobra was decanted out. Before any examination could take place, the snake had to be restrained, and once again Braam's catching tools were employed. He grabbed the snake's head firmly between his fingers and thumb, keeping the mouth closed. With the snake thus controlled, I was able to examine the wound. The snake appeared to have been bitten near the spine. There were also broken ribs at the bite site.

The dog is a powerful creature, and a bite from a Staffie can inflict terrible injuries. What we needed here was an X-ray to determine the extent of the wound and the damage to the spine. I felt that a sedative would not be a great idea because the snake was already severely stressed, and the sedative would just exacerbate matters. Braam undertook to hold the snake while I X-rayed it.

We dressed Braam in a lead apron and helped him put on a lead glove. He had to keep one hand free in order to hold the snake's head but was able to cover the free hand with the gloved one so as to protect himself from the X-rays.

We positioned the snake below the beam of the machine and placed it on an X-ray cassette. I set up the correct factors for the X-ray, and once this was done and all was ready, I pressed the button and fired off the machine. We took two exposures, one from the side and one from the top. In technical terms, these shots are called dorsoventral and lateral views. I then asked Braam to remove the snake and took the X-ray cassette to the dark room to develop. The entire procedure had taken a few short moments, and the developer took ninety seconds to develop the film. I came back from the dark room with the developed film and placed it on the light box for examination. What I saw really was not very promising at all.

Besides having a number of ribs fractured, the snake had a fractured vertebral column, or spine. This was clearly seen on both views. The spine is composed of a series of bones called vertebrae. There is a hole in each vertebra through which the spinal cord runs. Effectively, the bones form a long bony tube. If there is a fracture of the bones of the vertebral column, then there is often disruption or severance of the actual spine. This is a very severe injury, and the patient is paralyzed, usually for life. In this snake's case, the spine was completely severed from the bite of the dog. This snake would be paralyzed for the rest of its life.

We discussed the results of the X-rays and the various options that we had. Braam has a herpetarium and over the years has kept many injured snakes. He has rehabilitated them and successfully released them back into the wild. This option was discussed but in the end discarded, as I felt that the chances of this snake regaining the use of its lower body were pretty much zero. We could liberate the snake back into the environment as it was and let nature take its course, but this option was also discarded, as it was completely inhumane to do this. In addition to being inhumane, it was potentially very dangerous, because even though the snake was semi-paralyzed, it was still very poisonous, and given the fact that it now could not escape, it would become aggressive and even more dangerous.

The only thing left to do was to euthanize the unfortunate animal. Once we had made this decision, I asked Braam to restrain the snake once again, and I drew up sufficient euthanasia drug to do the deed. I usually try to inject snakes in the heart. I used a stethoscope to locate the heart, and once this was done, I injected 5 milliliters of the drug. Within a short time, the snake was dead.

Lying there still with eyes that had dulled in death, there was an air of melancholy that was almost palpable. This should never have happened. The dog was dead, the snake was dead, and all could have been avoided. I know that there is a lesson here somewhere; I just don't want to preach it.

Once the snake was still and at peace, Braam decided to use it to explain some facts about the Cape cobra. The snake was dead but still deadly. Even in death, if one accidentally allowed the teeth to prick an unprotected hand, there would be sufficient venom on the tooth itself to cause a problem. Carefully using steel forceps, Braam opened the mouth and showed me the very sharp but remarkably small teeth with poison dripping out of their tips. The actual teeth are hollow, like hypodermic needles. The snake bites its victim and injects poison into the prey via the needle-like teeth. Once the prey is dead, the snake swallows it whole. These snakes usually prey on rodents and other pests, and if not for the remarkable success of the snake as a rodent control measure, our domestic environment would be overrun by vermin. There is a place in the ecosystem for all of the living creatures on this planet.

We had to dispose of the body now that the snake was dead. Braam felt that the correct thing to do was to return it to the wild for nature to take its course. I felt that this was a good idea and gave it my support. The only thing that concerned me was that I did not want some animal or, even worse, some child to discover the corpse and possibly get injured. We decided to find a secluded place on the mountainside and place the body under a bush, where decomposition would occur rapidly. We placed the dead snake in a sack and drove up the slopes of Lion's Head to the top parking lot. From there we hiked the rest of the way to a secluded spot far away from the paths that are used by people and animals. Once we were happy that the spot was safe, we found a bush and tipped the dead snake out underneath it. We made sure that it was well covered by the bush and left the snake there.

As we left the mountainside that day, I looked around and was struck by something that I had not really focused on until that moment. There is a clear line between human habitat and the wild area occupied by animals. It is a line that is often crossed. We venture into nature, and sometimes wild animals enter into our domain. Whenever there is a clash between wild animals and us or our pets, there should be respect. With respect there can be coexistence. Without it, there can be only tragedy. We are the intruders here. We have occupied the mountainside. We are also the so-called intelligent species. It is up to us to set the example of how to cohabit with other species. If we do this with sensitivity, then we will all survive. If we do this without it, then our fellow inhabitants of this planet will be harmed, and we will be the poorer for it.

Many people asked me why Braam and I went to so much trouble to save a snake. "Why not just chop its head off?" they would say. Sometimes you just have to attend to the animal because you know no one else is going to help it. When an injured creature happens to come my way, I do not question its right to live. I do the best I can to make sure that it does live. If I was not meant to help, I have no doubt that it would not have ended up in my care. It's a philosophy that started with the seal in False Bay.

CHAPTER 15

Fish with the Bends

ONE OF THE STRANGE THINGS ABOUT US HUMANS IS THAT WHEN WE discover that animals can get the same conditions and diseases we do, we are surprised. Many times I've had owners express amazement that their animals developed liver, kidney, or heart failure, even cancer. But when I discovered that fish, who are at home in water, can actually develop the bends (a disease known as gas bubble disease), I must confess that even I was surprised. This is a disease more commonly associated with deep-sea divers.

My friend David Huchzermeyer, a veterinarian, invited me to observe him in action on a very interesting case that he was monitoring. He consults for a fish farm in the Leydenburg district in the north of South Africa, where there was an unusual situation. Fish were suffering from abscesses on their skin, and the various vets who had been called in were at their wit's end trying to cure the problem. Antibiotics had been administered but to no avail. When David was finally contacted, he not only examined the fish but also looked properly at the farm, the water supply, the management, the feed, and all the other factors that might play a role in the health and well-being of the fish.

I flew to Johannesburg and hired a Kombi to drive me, my director, George Mazarakis, and our film crew there. Leydenburg is about a four- or five-hour drive from Johannesburg, depending on how fast you travel. We set off for Leydenburg at four in the morning, and by just after eight, with nerves frayed, we arrived at our destination. When we arrived in this small town that is the center of the aquaculture industry in South Africa, we met David at his veterinary hospital. I had not seen him for about fifteen years and was surprised at how little he had changed. He still looked like the twenty-five-year-old young man that I remembered from school. He did, however, have an air of professionalism and competence about him that was missing when he was just a student. Since our gear was already loaded in the Kombi, he said that he would travel in his own vehicle, and we could follow him. I decided to travel with him and get some background information on the problem he had resolved.

While driving, David told me that fish on this farm we were visiting had been dying for a number of years, and the farmer was in serious trouble by the time David was called in to help. Up to 30 percent of his production was lost each year, and the farmer could not sustain another year like this. Most of the other vets called in had thought that there was an infection in the water, and numerous antibiotics had been prescribed, but nothing seemed to work. (The antibiotics are administered by dosing the water that the fish swim in.) David came in with a fresh set of eyes and more knowledge about fish than anyone else.

The water supply for the farm came from a waterfall that cascaded down the mountain for hundreds of feet before landing in a catchment pool. The water fell hard into the pool, resulting in super-aeration. The pool was also quite high above the ponds where the fish swam. There was a feeder pipe contributing to this extra aeration. The net result was that too much oxygen was being dissolved into the water. This excessively oxygenated water was "breathed" in by the fish through their gills; once in their bloodstream, the excess oxygen had nowhere to go other than to bubble out of the blood and form little bubbles in the gills and tissues. The result? Fish with the "bends." It took David quite a while and lots of thorough investigation to make this diagnosis.

David made recommendations based on his diagnosis and observations, and once these were instituted, the problem was solved. His recommendations were simple. Take the gate valve from the top of the feeder pipe and put it at the bottom, so that when the fish breathed the water, the amount of oxygen in it would be correct. This simple solution caused all the problems to clear up. Production rose by 30 percent, and David went from zero to hero.

After fixing the problem, David was called in on a weekly basis to monitor the trout on the farm. We were accompanying him on this weekly visit. There were still one or two fish per week that succumbed to the bends, but this was an acceptable and almost normal event. Provided that the numbers were kept in this range, all was well.

We arrived at our destination and climbed out of the vehicle. I looked around and was totally mesmerized by the beauty of the place. There were dozens of large, round ponds, each one measuring about 20 meters (66 feet) in diameter. These ponds were about 1 meter (3¼ feet) deep, and each one was filled with different-size fish, from fingerlings measuring a few centimeters in length to fully grown trout referred to as "table size," ready to be harvested and eaten. The ponds had green lawns surrounding them, and the entire farm was at the foot of a cliff 200 meters (656 feet) high. Cascading down the cliff was the offending waterfall, which was breathtakingly beautiful.

The view from my practice in Cape Town has to be one of the greatest in the world. I look over Table Bay, the city of Cape Town, Table Mountain, and the associated mountain ranges. I am spoiled, I know, but David's view of farmland, waterfalls, and gorgeous pools of fish glittering like diamonds in the sun sure is a close second.

So just how does one monitor a fish? Well, first you have to catch it, then you have to immobilize it for testing, and then you have to return it unharmed back to its environment. Let me tell you how this is done.

Fish can actually be anesthetized for up to a minute or so, and once asleep, they can be removed from the water and worked on. You add a special anesthetic agent to the water and wait while the fish swims around. You know when the fish is unconscious because it lies on its side.

When this occurs, you can remove it from the water and take your specimens. While I was watching him, David added the anesthetic agent to a large bin filled with water, then put one trout in the water. We waited. Within a few moments the fish was lying on its side. After wetting his hands well, David swiftly removed the fish from the water and placed it on a damp towel. He took a pair of scissors and snipped a small piece of gill tissue from underneath the gills, then took a microscope slide and gently scraped mucus off the fish's skin. Only a small amount of mucus was taken, because removing a lot of this slimy body covering can really harm the fish. The policy of doing minimal harm when examining any individual is employed here. David performed a quick visual inspection of the entire fish to make sure that there were no external ulcers. The fish was then returned to a bucket of fresh water with no anesthetic agent in it so that it could wake up and be brought back to the pond to join the other fish.

The specimens were then examined. The small snippet of gills was squashed onto a microscope slide and covered with a cover slip, and it and the mucus slide were examined under a microscope. Interestingly enough, if there are gas bubbles in the blood, they can be clearly seen in the gills when examined this way. In addition, if the fish is sick, there will be parasites on the skin that would not be found on a healthy fish. Although the entire process took just under a minute, the results of the examination were a sensitive barometer to the health of the pond. David looked at a few fish from the same pond, and from this he could infer the general health of the fish. Herd health implies that the vet examines a few individuals from the herd, flock, or, in this case, pond, in order to make inferences about the health of the entire group of animals that the vet is monitoring. The individual fish that we examined were in fact healthy, so the pond that we were examining was given a clean bill of health. David spoke to the owner of the farm and reported his findings to him. There seemed to be no problems that day.

Well, we had heard about gas bubble disease, we had seen how environmental factors could cause the problem, and we had witnessed the monitoring of the health of a pond, but we had still not seen an example of gas bubble disease. David finished his work at the trout farm, then told us that our next call was a koi farm a few kilometers away. There were fish there with active cases of gas bubble disease.

Trout and koi farmers have major philosophical differences when it came to the health and well-being of their respective fish. In the trout farm situation, an individual fish may sometimes be sacrificed to make a diagnosis, and in a pond of several thousand fish, one fish more or less is of little consequence. On a koi farm, however, individual fish may be worth up to 100,000 rand (currently about $13,590), so there is absolutely no sacrificing of individuals for the sake of the pond. Each fish is an individual and gets the full treatment. At the koi farm we were visiting, there were active cases of gas bubble disease, and these fish needed treatment on an individual basis.

Koi are raised for sale to the general public as pets. Owners have told me that each fish has a personality of its own. They can be tamed, hand fed, and will actually respond to individual signals. I have even heard of koi that come when they are called. Some like to be stroked, like cats.

Unlike the trout farm, most of the ponds on the koi farm are indoors. This is to maintain a constant environment, which will optimize survival. These fish individually have great financial worth and are treated very well. If an individual fish gets sick, it is isolated, monitored, and treated with the best medicine possible, usually by a fish specialist. That's where David comes in. He is a fish specialist and is often called out to handle koi.

When we arrived, the owner of the farm and his manager showed us into a large barnlike structure. To my surprise, once we were indoors, it was quite hot and humid. There were dozens of ponds, each with a different-size fish in it. The koi were divided into age groups, and the females were separated from the males. The females laid their eggs on artificial branches, which were left in the pond once the eggs were laid. The males were only allowed into the pond to fertilize the eggs. Once this was done, the adult fish were removed from the pond, and the fertilized eggs were allowed to hatch without the presence of adult fish to prey on them. This ensured optimum survival of the hatchlings.

We were then guided to the pond farthest from the entrance, which seemed to have the largest fish in it. Their colors were spectacular. Their individual monetary values were determined by the size of the fish and the rarity and pureness of their colors. The particular fish we were there to treat had magnificent orange and white skin. The white was very white, and the orange was like the setting sun. The manager of the farm used a special funnel-shaped net to capture the fish. It was allowed to swim head first into the canvas funnel, then the net was quickly lifted out, koi and all. The fish was gently decanted into a large bucket of fresh water. David added what he estimated to be the right dose of anesthetic to the water, and we waited for the fish to fall asleep.

After about ten minutes, the fish was still swimming sluggishly and was definitely not unconscious. David thought that even though the capture process was gentle, stress may have caused an adrenaline release. The adrenaline would counter the effect of the anesthetic, thus necessitating a higher dose. Reluctantly, he added a bit more to the water, and we waited for a few more minutes. This time the fish did go to sleep, and within two minutes our patient was lying on its side. The manager of the farm wet his hands and quickly but gently removed the fish from the bucket. They told me that this fish weighed about 5 kilograms (11 pounds). He placed the fish on a wet towel, and David ushered me over to show me what gas bubble disease looked like. He gently turned the fish onto its back, and just beneath the gills there were two ulcers, one on each side. The skin was broken and raw, and the lesions looked very sore. Clearly, this fish needed treatment.

How, you may wonder, does one apply topical treatment to a fish that swims in water? Well, David has used technology and an existing product to solve this problem. Baby diapers have a powdery clumping agent in them that forms a gel when wet. To this substance he adds antibiotics and any other remedies, then applies it to the ulcers. Once the powder is wet, it forms a sticky gel that stays on for hours in the water. The medicines are then absorbed and can help the fish. I wonder if the inventors of this product ever envisaged that it would be used to treat sick fish.

David applied the powder to the sick koi and made sure that the gel stuck to the slippery skin. The fish by now seemed to be waking up and started to wriggle. Then, with a flip of its tail, it effortlessly shed the hands that restrained it and jumped back into the water. David told us that the fish was actually so strong that without the help of the anesthetic, there was no way that we could have restrained or treated it.

Due to the chronic nature of the problem, the fish needed numerous applications of this special powder. Luckily, the prognosis is fairly good that fish treated this way will make a full recovery.

After finishing the treatment, we packed up our gear and prepared to leave for our drive back to Johannesburg.

We still had a four-hour journey ahead of us and were anxious to start. The owner of the koi farm, however, invited us to have a quick drink with him before we left. He had been kind enough to allow us to observe David at work, so we felt that the least we could do was to accept his invitation. While enjoying his refreshments at the farmhouse, he told us an astonishing story.

The farm used to have many of its ponds outside. Some of their largest and most valuable fish lived in these ponds. Aesthetically, this seemed to be a good option. The ponds were large, and the fish had the opportunity to live a more natural existence, exposed to fresh air, sunlight, and nature.

One night a few years ago, there was a violent storm and lots of lightning. When the staff arrived in the morning, they found one of the large ponds filled with dead fish. All the fish in the pond had been killed, and they had what looked like burn marks on them. The diagnosis was made that lightning had struck the pond, killing all the fish in it. This was a tragedy, not only of great financial proportions, but also because some of these fish were the tamest and oldest on the farm. The owner had actually befriended some of them himself, and he and his family wept at the death of these beautiful creatures.

After that, it was decided that the koi should be housed indoors. Away from nature, yes, but also away from the elements that sometimes can cause such a cruel blow.

Back in Johannesburg four hours later, I felt enriched to have been a part of this adventure. I had seen David in action, and I had learned the astonishing fact that aquatic creatures can suffer from the same debilitating and sometimes deadly disease that deep-sea divers get.

CHAPTER 16

The Croc Flock Doc

CROCODILES ARE CURRENTLY THE FAVORITE STAR OF MANY WILDLIFE television shows. I have great fascination for these creatures and therefore naturally gravitated toward the work of one of my teachers, Dr. Fritz Huchzermeyer, David's father. He offered to take me on a clinical case where he would handle and treat a crocodile. I wanted to observe firsthand how this was done and also wanted to ask many questions about these creatures from a veterinary perspective. After long conversations with him, I discovered that in fact one does not actually treat adult crocodiles clinically. I will explain more about this strange anomaly later.

Crocodiles are farmed now, and very successfully, I might add. Prior to their farming, the Nile crocodile was on the CITES endangered wildlife list. CITES stands for the Convention on International Trade in Endangered Species, and there are three CITES lists. Animals, such as cheetahs, that are most endangered are on the CITES 1 list. Animals on CITES 2 are less endangered than animals on CITES 1, and so on. The lists are management tools to help conserve endangered species. Nile crocodiles were on CITES 3 at one point but now are off the list. The farming of crocodiles for both their meat and skins has been so successful that their numbers are now well within the range that ensures survival. There are some massive farming enterprises in southern Africa, and this is one of the few instances where commercial interests and wildlife interests have led to the survival of a species.

Dr. Huchzermeyer was a consultant to numerous crocodile farms and told me that his main function there was to monitor herd health. He offered to take me along to two farms and show me what he did there. The main activity in managing the croc flock was to draw blood regularly from young crocodiles and monitor certain parameters that indicated whether or not the animals were stressed. The whole idea here is to minimize stress and maximize growth and production.

We met at his practice on the eastern outskirts of Pretoria early one morning and drove some 50 kilometers (31 miles) to the first farm. The farm consisted of two general areas. There were large barns, where the young crocs were kept indoors in ponds. The conditions in these indoor paddocks were kept constant to ensure that the young crocodiles were raised in optimum conditions. The second general area was where the adult crocodiles were kept. This area was a very large man-made lake that must have measured some 200 meters (656 feet) in diameter. A brick wall circled the entire lake. The lake was in the open air and was surrounded by a concrete "shore." There were also islands in the lake. Around the perimeter of the lake, the "shoreline" sloped gently into the water. On the shoreline, against the perimeter wall, there were numerous pens with earth flooring. This was where the female crocodiles laid their eggs. Low walls separated the pens from each other, and an individual crocodile was able to lay her eggs in peace once inside her pen. The pens were also numbered to facilitate identification.

The females laid eggs at night, then buried the eggs in the sand just under the surface of the pen. The laying pens were monitored daily, and once eggs were laid, they were removed from the pens and placed in the hatchery. Dr. Huchzermeyer jokingly told us that the highest paid individual on the farm was the man who removed the eggs from the nests in the morning. In fact, there were two men involved in this task, one with a stick to fend off the attention of any crocodile close by, and the other to harvest the eggs. The crocodiles left their nests during the day and retreated to the water, so harvesting the eggs was not the extremely dangerous task we initially thought it was.

The life span of a crocodile is very similar to the life span of a human. They live to between seventy and eighty years of age. They are small and relatively helpless at birth. They undergo puberty at between ten and thirteen years of age. They grow longer until they reach the age of about eighteen or twenty, when they hit their breeding prime. They are then regarded as adults. From here on they don't get longer, just fatter. They become old and cranky from their midforties on.

The similarity in life stages between crocs and humans is almost laughable.

Crocs make very good parents, and unlike other reptiles, they don't abandon their young, but actually look after them and guard them during their infancy. The similarity to birds is notable. Once the young crocodiles reach a certain length, they are chased away by the adults, but this can take a few years before it happens. They seem to live in flocks, similar to birds. In fact, Dr. Huchzermeyer repeated often that their behavior was remarkably similar to birds'. Birds are thought to be the modern descendants of dinosaurs, and crocodiles are thought to be the only remaining survivors from that period.

Crocodiles have a number of ways of moving. They can swim in the water using their webbed feet and powerful tails to propel them. They slither on mud and sand using their legs to paddle their bodies forward. When they do this, they leave the characteristic "slide" marks that identify the fact that crocs have been around. They can walk with their bodies elevated above the ground, such as when they waddle onto sandy beaches to bask in the sun. This is their chosen gait for moving around on land when they are not in a hurry. Lastly, they can gallop. When hunting, they can observe their prey from underwater, with just their eyes and nostrils sticking out of the water. Then, when they judge the time to be right, they give a sudden, very powerful thrash of their tail and launch themselves at full gallop toward their hapless prey at about 40 kilometers (25 miles) an hour. This means that if the prey is within 10 meters (33 feet) of the edge of the pond, the croc will cover that distance in a second. This is not enough time for escape, and their success rate at hunting for prey in this manner is very high. Tribal fishermen occasionally fall prey to a croc that launches itself in this manner. The poor human just does not have the time to move out of the way. If the croc is large enough, it will be able to drag the person down, and a drowning will occur. These people are seldom found again. Crocodiles have lairs underwater in submerged caves and are thought to store their prey there, allowing the flesh to rot before consuming the meat. What a dreadful way to meet one's end!

Crocs breathe air through their nostrils, but they are able to slow their heart and respiration rate down so dramatically that under certain circumstances, they can remain underwater for two hours without breathing. They can also compress the volume of air in their lungs, so that this air acts as a diving chamber. When the chamber is expanded, the croc will rise to the surface, and when compressed, the croc will sink below the surface. This is a voluntary action and is why they are able to rise or submerge silently with no movement of any visible part of their bodies.

In summer, they feed once a week, but in the cold of winter, their metabolism slows down so dramatically that they actually don't need food for months on end. If they feed in winter, the food can rot in their intestines, causing their death.

They regulate their body temperature by basking in the sun to warm up. If they overheat, they do what is called "gaping." They lie with their mouths open, and in this way they get rid of excess heat. They also obviously go into water if it gets too hot. In the cool of the morning, they are sluggish and cannot move fast, so they don't hunt early. They are most dangerous during the warm part of the day, when their bodies have warmed up and they can move fastest.

By the time these animals exhibit signs of disease, they are generally too sick to survive. There is also the practical problem of clinically examining and treating these large, strong reptiles. The best form of care for these animals is to try to monitor the health of the entire "flock" of crocs and to ensure that they live in a stress-free and healthy environment. In this way, disease is prevented, because it is difficult if not impossible to actually cure a sick croc.

Dr. Huchzermeyer told us all these fascinating facts while we were standing on an island in the middle of the croc pond. The pond was filled with well over two hundred crocodiles, the smallest of which must have been 3 meters (10 feet). They lazed on the shore, they swam silently in the water, and they nested in their enclosures. In fact, wherever we looked, there were crocodiles. The island we stood on was linked to the outside of the enclosure by a walkway over the water, and a croc-proof fence surrounded our island. This was the service area that was used to clean and maintain the filter equipment for the pond.

While standing and talking to the croc doc, my foot protruded slightly over the walkway and the water. Dr. Huchzermeyer suddenly noticed this and quickly pulled me away from the edge. Just as he did this, a large croc emerged beneath me. It had clearly seen my foot sticking out and had come over to investigate. Dr. Huchzermeyer told me that if it had launched itself at me, I would not have had time to pull my leg away, and we may have had a problem. Needless to say, I kept well clear of the edge after that.

Once we had seen the adult animals, we were taken to the second farm, about a twenty-minute drive away. There we had the chance to examine and handle the young crocs. We were also taken into a hatchery to look at eggs and hatchlings. But the climax of this visit was feeding the crocs. If I thought that the adults were interesting, they paled into insignificance when compared with the young crocodiles.

One must not forget that this is a farming enterprise. The farm produces a product, namely, crocodile skins and meat. This means that somewhere along the line, the animals are slaughtered and processed into a product that can be sold. Individuals have a commercial value, so their production must be optimized. This means that they must be housed and fed in such a manner as to maximize growth and minimize stress. To achieve this, the young crocs are kept indoors in temperature-regulated barns in dark conditions. Now, this is not as bad as it sounds, because in the wild, when crocs are young, they tend to gather together in dark places that are moist and warm and close to water. They also gather together because there is safety in numbers. Knowing this and having been briefed by Dr. Huchzermeyer about the warm, fetid conditions in the barns, I was still not prepared for what assailed my senses.

Earlier in my career as a vet, I had once made a house call to an eccentric woman living in Brighton, England. I discovered that she kept about one hundred cats in her house and allowed them to defecate and urinate everywhere. The stench was indescribable. Well, the smell in the croc barn was much worse than that. Imagine the filthiest urinal you've ever seen on a very hot day. Multiply that by a very large number, and you'll have some inkling of the smell that we had to endure while working in the barn.

Inside the barn were a number of pens, each measuring about 20 by 20 meters (66 by 66 feet). The pens were concrete and had a shelved concrete floor filled with water, so that the young crocs could bask on the "banks" partially submerged. They were also able to float in the water in a strange upright position. They stood on their back legs and tail, with their front legs and head floating in the water. This appeared to be an upright position, and the water in this way supported the crocs with just their heads out. The light was low, and the air was uncomfortably warm, about 38° Celsius (100° Fahrenheit), I was told. Each pond housed between two hundred and three hundred baby crocodiles. We had to bring extra lighting into the barn so we were able to illuminate the place and have a good look around. The young crocs did not like the light and started to move away from it. We all had to be very quiet, and any talking was done sotto voce.

One of the handlers who work on the farm climbed into the pond that we were standing near. It was the one closest to the front door, which stood ajar, allowing a trickle of fresh air to seep inside. He approached the writhing mass of crocodiles carefully so as not to startle them. They did seem anxious and started to move away from him. He had obviously done this before, because, with a swift lunge, he managed to grab one croc behind the head and by the tail. Thus restrained, the croc immediately gave up the fight and allowed itself to be carried to where Dr. Huchzermeyer waited. We then carried the croc outside, where the croc doc prepared to take a blood sample. There is a large tail vein that runs along the back of the animal, and this is the one used to sample blood. The handler restrained the croc, while Dr. Huchzermeyer took a hypodermic needle and a syringe and positioned himself behind the croc. The handler then bent the tail down, and Dr. Huchzermeyer inserted the needle in the correct spot where the tail was flexed. The blood flowed into the collecting tube, and without too much fuss, we obtained our sample.

This sample was then sent to a laboratory, and numerous parameters were examined. Under specific adverse conditions associated with stress, certain bacteria start to flourish. If they are detected, then it would be safe to assume that all the animals are stressed. The whole process took under thirty seconds, and the patient was then returned to its pond without suffering any apparent ill effects.

Gratefully, we finished our work in the barns, and gasping, we stumbled outside. We were then taken to the hatchery. I was shown the egg incubation racks where there were hundreds of eggs being incubated. One could control the sex of the crocodile hatching by regulating the temperature of the incubation. At a certain temperature, males were hatched, and at another temperature, females would hatch. This means that the genetic potential for both sexes was in each egg, but depending on the temperature, one could choose the gender desired. This had some commercial value, in that females seemed to grow better in the farming environment.

I was given an egg and turned it over in my hands to examine it. Another handler approached us carrying a baby crocodile that had just hatched. This little creature was about 15 centimeters (6 inches) long and glistened with the fluids from the yolk sac. This appeared as a small yellow blob underneath the baby croc on its abdomen, where the belly button would have been. The little croc was mobile and able to emit a small clicking and squeaking sound. This attracts the mother to the nest when the young hatch. At one time the Nile crocodile had a reputation for eating its young. This was a mistake that was made by early observations of their behavior. What in fact happens is that even before they hatch, the hatchlings emit this vocalization. This attracts the mother croc back to the nest, and she then digs up the nest and will even crack eggs that are not yet hatched. She will then take the babies in her mouth and transport them to the water. The survival rate of baby crocs hatched in the wild is quite high due to the diligence of the mother and her ability to transport the babies safely in her rather fearsome mouth. The adult crocs will also defend their young from predators, such as monitor lizards, who fancy both crocodile eggs and newly hatched babies as part of their diet.

The little creature nestled in my hand and moved about without fear. I hoped that it would not imprint on me. They imprint on the first moving creature that comes their way. This is usually the mother. In this way, a parental bond is established. Well, if it thought I was its mother, it was in for a surprise. I marveled that this small being could one day be big enough to make a quick snack out of someone my size.

We finished in the hatchery and were then told by the handlers that today was feeding day for the adults in the breeding pond on this farm. We were in luck, because this was a spectacular sight. The crocs are fed on chicken meat that is obtained from a nearby chicken farm. The handlers had two wheelbarrows filled with frozen chicken parts, and we followed them to the breeding pond. I followed the handlers into a large enclosure, where there was a big pool. There did not seem to be anything in the pool, just a glassy surface. The handlers parked their wheelbarrows about 5 meters (5 yards) from the edge and then whistled loudly. The next instant pandemonium broke out. Adult crocodiles erupted from the pool and came charging hell-bent toward us. They reached the bank of the pond, and for a heart-stopping moment I thought I was in real trouble, but they stopped there and waited. I got the impression that they were like dogs waiting to be fed. This ritual had happened so many times that the crocodiles knew the whistle preceded a feed, and they also had acquired the habit of waiting for their food on the edge of the pond. The handlers started throwing chickens to these animals. The crocs caught the chickens in midair and with an audible gulp, swallowed them. I had to get in on the action and grabbed a chicken in each hand and tossed them to the waiting crocs. These adult crocs were massive, some in excess of 6 meters (20 feet) long and nearly 2 meters (7 feet) wide. An adult can weigh well over 270 kilograms (595 pounds), with some individuals being estimated at over 450 kilograms (990 pounds). I have fed many animals in my life, but this had to be the high point of my animal-feeding career. The largest of them consumed about ten or twelve chickens and then seemed to be satisfied. Once satiated, the crocs slid back into the pond to cool off and digest.

Within the space of an hour, I had held a crocodile egg, cradled a newly hatched baby in my hands, handled meter-long young animals, and fed adults so large that they could have made a meal of me. The sheer size and number of crocodiles that we saw that day, combined with the thrill of the potential danger that these massive animals represented, will be a memory that I will carry to my dying day.

CHAPTER 17

A Ball of Spikes Unrolls

A HEDGEHOG IS A BALL OF MORE THAN SEVEN THOUSAND SPINES, FOUR legs, and a small tail. Its favorite habitats are the edges of forests, gardens, and parks. Hedgehogs are active at night, resting between five in the morning and eight in the evening, although I would not set my watch by their timetable. They are rather solitary creatures, and they will easily start fighting with each other if they meet up at night. Their life span is from six to ten years.

Their sight and hearing are rather good, but their sense of smell is excellent. A hedgehog's nose is always wet and sniffing about. Even a worm hidden 3 centimeters (1 inch) under the ground will not be safe from a hedgehog. Hedgehogs are especially welcome by passionate gardeners, as they manage to keep garden parasites down to a minimum. Hedgehogs eat worms, insects (including bees and spiders), snakes, and mice. In critical situations, they will also eat berries. The hedgehog has great physical strength, considering its size. It can crawl through very narrow places, it is a real long-distance walker, it is adept at running quite fast, and it is also an accomplished swimmer.

Those who have read the charming tales written by Beatrix Potter will be familiar with that dear little character Miss Tiggywinkle, a very famous hedgehog who wears an apron and drinks tea. Most people think of the hedgehog as residing in Great Britain and Europe, but the hedgehog is also present in South Africa. They live in and around cities, in the bush, and in less-developed areas. If your house has a green lawn around it, or you live near a golf course, there are probably hedgehogs near you. Unfortunately, when these cute little creatures come into contact with pet dogs, they usually don't make out well. Hedgehogs defend themselves by rolling up into tight little balls of spikes. If the dog is large enough, however, the hedgehog's standard defense mechanism is of no use, and usually they are killed outright. On rare occasions an injured hedgehog may end up needing veterinary care.

One afternoon back in 1998, I was visiting a friend of mine, Dr. Leon Louw. We had been to the farm where the gemsboks were battling for survival, and on our way back we stopped at the Pretoria Zoo, as Leon was one of the vets working there. This is a world-class facility and truly is one of the treasures of South Africa. The zoo is vast and magnificent. Keeping the animals well and healthy is the zoo's mission. The enclosures are built with sensitivity to the animals' needs and with due consideration to their natural environment. The success of a zoo is measured by the reproductive success of its animals. By this and any other standard, the

Pretoria Zoo is a great success. The zoo had just recently been successful in breeding a rare subspecies of lion known as the white lion of Timbavati. These lions have a heritable genetic mutation causing their coats to be a very light cream instead of the usual darker color typical of African lions.

While we were there, a hedgehog was brought in for attention. It had strayed too close to civilization and had been cornered and mauled by a dog. The dog's owner was kind enough to catch the little chap and bring it to the zoo, where they have a small but busy wildlife rescue unit. This is where my friend and colleague Leon comes into the picture.

We followed Leon to the treatment rooms and were presented with a small ball of spikes. It was hard to believe that this prickly thing was actually a living creature. A hedgehog's spikes are very hard, and if you were to try to unravel it, it would just curl up tighter. The only way to examine this animal was to inject it with a powerful sedative that would render it unconscious. We would also be able to tell if it was indeed a "little chap."

I put on a set of heavy leather gloves to handle the hedgehog, while Leon prepared a syringe filled with anesthetic agent. Within six minutes of being injected, the ball slowly uncurled itself as it drifted off to slumber on its back. The hedgehog looked like the hero of countless children's fairy tales, just stepped out of a book. It was about 15 centimeters (6 inches) long with tiny paws, a pointed nose, and long bristles for whiskers.

Once it had unwound like this, we noted some superficial wounds on its back, where the dog had bitten it. There was also a deep laceration that needed suturing. Leon proceeded to clean and disinfect the wound and to remove some of the necrotic tissue surrounding it. It looked like this wound had been inflicted a day or so ago. There was swelling and inflammation but nothing too serious. After cleaning the area with disinfectant and cotton balls, Leon brought out the suture pack and instruments. It was not possible to shave the area, which is what would usually be done to a surgical site. This was because our razor would not cut the spikes. Leon placed a few sutures in the wound and closed it up. Then he applied some antibiotic paste to the wound and injected a small amount of antibiotic. The little chap was then hospitalized in a heated cage and allowed to wake up by himself.

Easily stressed by captivity and confinement, wild animals generally don't respond well to a hospital situation. The best course of action is to return them to their natural environment as quickly as possible. Our hedgehog would be examined again in twenty-four hours. After this examination, if there were no further problems, he would be returned to the wild. Our little chap was found to be remarkably well, considering his ordeal. The zoo made sure that he was released in an area that was sparsely populated with humans and dogs, so that his chance of survival in the wild was maximized.

Chapter 18

Pain in the Neck

ONE DAY, MY GOOD FRIEND AND COLLEAGUE PETER ROGERS CALLED TO make me an offer I couldn't refuse. He informed me about a cheetah that needed attention at the game reserve where he served as wildlife vet at Hoedspruit. Like many game reserve animals, this cheetah had a radio collar around its neck. In some cases, these collars can be unwieldy and a real hindrance to the animal. If a cheetah that weighs 45 kilograms (99 pounds) has a collar that can weigh up to 5 kilograms (11 pounds), then this extra weight can seriously disrupt the cheetah's ability to hunt effectively. Because of these and other reasons, the game reserve wanted the collar removed. Peter was called in to dart the cheetah, remove the collar, and surgically implant the new tracking device into its abdomen. This was a very uncommon procedure at the time, so I jumped at the opportunity.

I caught a flight from Cape Town to Johannesburg, then a connecting flight to Hoedspruit. Hoedspruit is a small town nestled between the foothills of the Drakensberg Mountains to the west and Kruger National Park to the east. There is a mix of cultures living there, but all the inhabitants are involved somehow in the game industry, whether by owning land or by performing a service to the people or animals (both wild and tame) living in the area.

As I disembarked from the plane, I felt the warm, dry wind of the lowveld. The color scheme of the bush always evokes a line from one of my favorite poems. Translated from Afrikaans, this line describes "the blue and the blond" ("*die blou en die blond*") of the bushveld. The grass is dry and blond, and the sky is a piercing blue. It is quite a sight to behold.

The surgery that the cheetah was going to have to undergo was an elective operation and had been scheduled for the day following our arrival. Once again I was accompanied by a film crew. There was the cameraman, Mike Zidel, as well as a sound man. We therefore had the opportunity to settle into our lodgings and take the afternoon off to familiarize ourselves with the territory. We were staying in a camp at Kapama, the wildlife reserve where Peter worked.

Peter had a wildlife hospital situated on Kapama. There is an area on this reserve that is dedicated to conservation of endangered species, such as Lente Roode's Cheetah Project. That first afternoon we took the opportunity to visit the area. We climbed into an open Land Rover and were driven around by a game warden who showed us the various species that were being bred there.

The next morning, we awoke before first light. With only a coffee and a rusk to fortify ourselves, we drove our Kombi to Peter's wildlife hospital, where we loaded the game vehicle and headed for the Karongwe reserve, a private park 20 kilometers (12 miles) from Phalaborwa and about 60 kilometers (37 miles) from where we were based. This was where our cheetah, who was going to have his state-of-the-art implant, lived, and this was to be the site of our adventure.

The Karongwe reserve is bordered by tribal trust land owned by indigenous farmers. This is a danger zone for cheetahs. The tribal landowners shoot any cheetahs that stray onto their land. It is their perception that cheetahs kill their livestock. It is extremely unlikely that a 45- to 50-kilogram (99- to 110-pound) cheetah would be able to take down a fully grown cow that may weigh hundreds of kilograms, so this perception was not based on reality. It would, however, be possible for cheetahs to prey on calves, so the policy of collaring and monitoring their whereabouts was a solution that made everyone happy. Besides, it was extremely rare that the cheetahs would stray onto the farmers' land because of the enormous efforts made by the rangers in their attempt to prevent just this.

The radio collars were heavy enough to disturb a cheetah's balance while hunting. They also chafed the animal's neck and caused severe irritation. For these reasons, and because implants were aesthetically more acceptable from a tourist's point of view, we had elected to go for the implant. A collared animal is visually jarring to a tourist who has come to see wild Africa.

Kaylee Owen lived on Karongwe and was conducting a research project at the reserve. She had initially arrived on the reserve as a student but eventually became part of the game ranger staff, and she conducted useful research there as well. She was in charge of the collaring and tracking program. Her aim was to discover more about the cheetahs' habits and whereabouts. With her help, we set off to locate our patient. This should have been simple, but this was Africa. The bush was so dense that we could have been 5 meters (5 yards) away from the cheetahs and not noticed them. I could literally have stumbled over any number of wild animals lying quietly in the bush.

Often while walking through the bush tracking a wild animal, I have pondered my actions. I have been charged by lions and an elephant and have often wished that I was safely back home. Once the dangerous moment is over, though, I realize how lucky I am to be a part of all of this. On the cheetah hunt, my pulse was racing, not only from the brisk walk, but also because of the palpable sense of danger. The fact that an armed ranger accompanied us was small comfort.

The radio collar suddenly emitted a signal to our tracking device, which meant that the cheetahs were close by. Unfortunately, they were one step ahead of us on that hot, dusty morning, and the heat was getting to us all. I was caked in sweat and longed for water. After about an hour of this cat-and-mouse game, the cheetahs finally settled under the shade of some trees. They too eventually needed some respite. It was at this point that we thought we had our chance. All the while that we had tracked the animals, Peter had carried his dart gun, loaded and primed to shoot in an instant. Now, with our quarry settled, Peter prepared to dart his patient. He was familiar with this particular cheetah, a male, and knew approximately how much he weighed. This information is important in working out the dose of anesthetic agent used in the dart. You want to put the cheetah to sleep quickly and keep it asleep long enough to do the job.

With very little noise, Peter carefully tested the wind to be sure that we were downwind. The animals knew we were there, but extra precaution could do no harm. Once satisfied that his careful approach would not startle them, he managed to get within shooting distance. This was about 20 meters (22 yards) in this case. With an almost casual air, he lifted the dart rifle to his left shoulder, took aim, and fired the dart. With a sharp sound like air being blasted through your teeth, the pink-tasseled dart flew and embedded itself into the hindquarters of the cheetah. The impact of the dart startled him, and he sprang off. We are always concerned that the animal may take flight and run after being darted. In this case, however, the radio collar would help in locating him once he was asleep. The dart we used that day contained a combination of two drugs, Domitor and ketamine. This would put the cheetah to sleep in six minutes and keep him safely anesthetized and down for up to forty-five minutes. Fortunately, the cheetah ran only a few paces; he settled down under a nearby tree and went uneventfully to sleep.

The rangers clapped and shooed the other cheetahs away as if they were harmless pigeons in the park. Cheetahs generally are not aggressive animals, and it is rare that they would view a human as food. They hunt animals that are smaller than they are, and a human does not quite fit the bill, at least not an adult human. Besides, these cheetahs were habituated to people.

We squatted down to examine the sleeping cheetah. There was some routine maintenance work to be done. First, the dart had to be removed. We used a scalpel blade to make a small nick just next to the barbed dart. The dart was then gently pulled through this incision, and once out, the hole was filled with an antibiotic paste. It is routine for a vet to check vital signs on an unconscious patient before anything else is done. We performed our preop check there and then, under the shade of an African tree. Once we were certain that our patient was stable and soundly asleep, we made arrangements to move him to the chosen site. We had a mat with handles on either side to use to carry him to his destination. We carefully placed the sleeping cheetah onto this mat. In the process, we had to roll him over. This simple act presented a particular challenge, as the cheetah seemed to have a full belly. If a cheetah is rolled over while his belly is full, it is possible for the stomach to twist in the abdomen, causing a condition known as gastric torsion, which can be life-threatening. Making absolutely sure that no adverse reactions occurred, we rolled the cheetah onto the mat and carried it to a clearing where the bush operating theater had been set up. The vehicles had been brought to the clearing, and trestle tables had been set up to act as an operating table and instrument trolley. The operating table was padded with a mattress and covered with green surgical drapes that had previously been sterilized.

Even in the bush, basic principles apply. The first thing a vet does with an anesthetized patient is to carefully monitor him and ensure that all the vital signs are within normal parameters. We had already done a preop examination on our cheetah. Once he was lying on our bush operating table, this examination was performed again. We set up an intravenous drip as a precaution. This ensured that we had a patent vein that we could use in the event of an emergency. Little did we realize just how fortunate taking this precaution would be. We monitored his temperature, pulse, and respiration as well. We were now sure that the sleeping cheetah was stable, and the next phase of the operation could start. While we were busy getting the cheetah ready for surgery, Phillip, the game ranger, was busy removing the bulky radio collar from the cheetah's neck using a pair of pliers to unscrew the nuts and bolts that kept it on. Underneath the collar, his fur was badly chafed away, and the skin was thickened and hard with calluses. I knew he would be much happier without the collar.

Next, we positioned the sleeping cheetah on his back and tied him in position for surgery. We used ropes to extend his hind legs so that his belly was clearly exposed. We then used water and soap and a razor to shave all the coarse hair off his belly. Once this task was completed, we scrubbed his belly with water and a special sterilizing fluid called chlorhexidine. This is the same product used to sterilize skin in human surgery. While I was scrubbing the cheetah's skin, Peter was busy scrubbing his own hands with water and chlorhexidine as well. He then gloved his hands using sterile surgical gloves. I unwrapped his sterile instruments from their transport wrapping, and Peter inserted his hands into the sterile wrapping to remove the instruments wrapped in green surgical cloth. All this was done very carefully to avoid contamination. Wrapped up with the sterile instruments was a sterile, fenestrated drape. This was opened and placed over the scrubbed belly. The drape has a square hole cut into it through which the surgery takes place.

This is not a very complicated piece of surgery. It involves opening the abdomen and gently inserting the radio transmitter implant. The implant itself is small, about 10 centimeters (4 inches) long and about 5 centimeters (2 inches) in diameter, and once implanted it sits in the caudal part of the abdomen just like a lump of feces. To give you some idea of its dimensions, it is about the length of your palm, and if you place your finger and thumb together and make a circle of them, the transmitter will fit through that hole snugly. It weighs about 150 grams (5 ounces). It is completely harmless and causes no side effects at all. The battery powering the transmitter lasts over two years. Prior to its insertion, it had been soaking in chlorhexidine and was completely sterile.

After gently sliding the implant into the abdomen, Peter started to close up the incision using dissolvable sutures in the muscular layer. As he was doing this, the cheetah began to stir. The drug was supposed to keep the animal soundly asleep for about forty-five minutes, but we had only been at it for about twenty. We immediately called for assistance from the people surrounding us who were viewing the surgery. They physically restrained the cheetah, and I dashed for Peter's drug box and took out the bottle of anesthetic agent. Luckily, we had set up a drip line, so we had instant access to a vein. I drew up a dose of anesthetic and quickly injected it into the vein of the now thrashing cheetah. An intravenous dose of anesthetic is very rapid in its action, and within five seconds, the animal once again succumbed. In this short time, however, we nearly had a catastrophe. The operating table almost tipped over, and the sterile drapes were tossed all around. Had it not been for the meticulous preparation done before surgery, we might have had a major problem.

The surgical site's sterility had been compromised, and we had to scrub, drape, and glove again. Once this was done, Peter continued with the abdominal closure. The muscular layer was sutured closed, and he used the same suture material for the skin. The suture material, PDS, takes about forty days to dissolve. Including the ten-minute interruption, the surgery had taken about twenty-five minutes from first cut to last suture. Once the last suture was placed, our sterile gloves were removed and the drapes taken off. The cheetah's belly was sprayed with a disinfectant, and routine antibiotics were administered. The drip was removed, and the antidote to the anesthetic was administered. This would wake the cheetah up within about five minutes.

After the operation was completed, we had the opportunity to discuss some of the theoretical considerations as to why the cheetah woke up. There was nothing wrong with the preparations for surgery, and the dose of drug was correct. We had to put it down to an idiosyncratic drug reaction. It is a very rare phenomenon, but it does occur. Every once in a while an animal has an adverse reaction to a drug. Usually the anesthetic is deeper than planned for the given dose, but in this case, it lasted for only half the prescribed time. Had it not been for the professional preparation and meticulous attention to detail that Peter is renowned for, we may have had the very unpleasant experience of a wild animal escaping from an operating table with a surgical wound still in its abdomen. We had been sweating a little before this operation; after its completion, we were all soaked.

When we were done, Kaylee Owen switched on her tracking device and tuned it in to the radio implant signal just placed in the cheetah's belly. It was giving out a steady, slow signal, indicating a strong battery that would last for in excess of two years. The tracking monitor that she used had twenty different frequencies and could be used to monitor twenty animals with radio collars or implants. She just had to tune the monitor in to the frequency of the chosen transmitter. This is an invaluable tool in the bush when trying to locate the whereabouts of wild animals. It is also one of the reasons why private game reserves can almost guarantee that their guests will see the "Big Five" within a short time of arriving at the reserve. This is a well-kept secret, and if you don't tell, neither will I. It somehow spoils the romance of seeing all these wonderful animals so quickly on the first day of your safari when you know that the animals' whereabouts are carefully monitored with state-of-the-art equipment.

We transferred the cheetah to a shady spot 50 meters (55 yards) away using the transporting mattress with handles again. We then sat quietly and watched him wake up. Slowly the cheetah arose, shaking his head. We had to make sure that there were no other animals around as he regained consciousness. This would have served as a perfect opportunity for an enemy cheetah to take advantage of our patient in his vulnerable state and tackle him. We guarded him while he took a few tentative steps. The antidote, however, works quickly, and within minutes he was fully awake and striding gracefully. The next day we tracked him again just to make sure he had suffered no ill effects from the surgery. We discovered to our delight that he and another cheetah had already hunted successfully. I found it amazing that within a few hours after abdominal surgery, the cheetah could hunt. This proved to me once again that it had been a sterile and successful piece of surgery that didn't in any way harm the cheetah. It was also a tribute to the resilience of the wild inhabitants of this planet in contrast to us. Had a human had the same surgery, the recovery period would have been weeks. With a wild animal, the recovery period is hours. The cynic in me says that it is our human brains that retard our recovery. If we undergo a medical procedure, we expect to be sore, and this becomes a self-fulfilling prophecy. Animals, however, have no expectation of pain, and if it happens, they stoically get on with their lives. I think this is philosophically a far better way to go about one's business.

That night our team decided to celebrate at the little restaurant in the old Hoedspruit railway station. The food was good, the wine was palatable, the cigar tasted great, but the satisfaction of a job well done was the feeling that I was most contented with.

CHAPTER 19

Tuberculosis Testing in Lions

A VET PLAYS A VERY IMPORTANT ROLE IN PUBLIC HEALTH, INCLUDING THE prevention of the spread of diseases from animals to humans or vice versa. Diseases that are classically associated with humans can become serious killers of animals if they get into the animal population as well. Tuberculosis has been around for a long time and has killed many millions of people. Probably more people have died of TB on the African continent than any other single disease, including AIDS; only time will tell whether or not AIDS will take over this unenviable record. What is not widely known, however, is that the wild and domestic animals of Africa also can contract TB, and it is fatal for them too.

There are two strains of *Mycobacterium* that cause TB; one is called *Mycobacterium bovis* and the other *Mycobacterium tuberculosis.* One of the reasons we pasteurize milk is to kill these two strains. *Mycobacterium bovis* is transmitted from infected cattle to humans via their milk and causes about 10 percent of TB in humans; the other 90 percent is caused by *Mycobacterium tuberculosis.* If you drink unpasteurized milk from a cow that is infected with *Mycobacterium bovis* or *tuberculosis,* then you will probably contract TB. Testing milk cow herds for TB is in fact a major part of a cattle vet's work. Primates that are kept in zoos also suffer from TB. This strange fact is caused by humans actually spitting at these innocent captive animals through the wire fences of their cages. If the person doing the spitting is infected with TB, that is sufficient to cause the disease in these captive animals. What strange and unkind creatures some of us humans are!

Tuberculosis has entered the wild animal population in a very interesting way. Domestic cattle infected with TB have grazed on the same pastures with wild buffalo in areas adjacent to Kruger National Park. The buffalo have then become infected via contact with these cattle because the disease is spread through infected saliva or sputum. Grazing on an area contaminated by the sputum of an infected cow is sufficient to cause the disease. Infected animals will cough, and their saliva will land on buffalo or the grass being grazed by buffalo, and in this way the disease spreads. The infected buffalo become weak, and these are the ones that will more commonly fall prey to a predator such as a lion. The lions eat the infected animal, and they in turn become infected. They will then spread TB into their own population, and so the cycle goes on. TB is now rife in the wild animals of Africa, and it is a major problem. Death among wildlife due to TB is now an all too common occurrence. Carrion eaters such as hyenas may then eat a predator that has died from TB. Once this happens, the disease spreads into the hyena population. One can see just how easily this highly infectious disease spreads.

There are programs conducted by the state to at least control the spread of this disease. All wild animals on game reserves that are to be moved from one reserve to another must be tested for TB. If they are found to be positive, then they must be culled and their herd mates quarantined. This process would continue until the entire population of affected animals has been culled or proven TB free. Needless to say, this is a major problem for the reserve owners, and it can have serious economic implications for the game reserve. There are programs conducted at various private and state-run game reserves to try to breed TB-free buffalo and lions. The success of these programs has yet to be determined.

The population of wild lions on the Thornybush game reserve had expanded to such a degree that there were now too many lions in too small a place. Lions are skilled predators, and given sufficient prey on which to feed, they will breed very successfully. Once there are too many lions for a particular area, they are sold off to other reserves wishing to introduce this alpha predator into their ecosystem.

Before moving any wild animals, especially lions, that may have preyed upon infected buffalo or any other infected game animals, these animals must be tested for tuberculosis. This involves a general anesthetic and the administration of a special TB test.

There were four lions at Thornybush that were scheduled to be sold toward the end of one late October. They had to be tested prior to the sale. If they were negative, they could go to their new home, but if they tested positive, they would be culled. This is a very serious test with dire consequences for the animals that test positive. Everyone involved in this kind of testing is usually very somber and tense. If the animals prove to be negative, there is cause for joy and celebration, but if they test positive, the mood turns very dark. It's ironic that magnificent animals strong enough to kill almost any animal they meet in the wild are destroyed because of a microorganism too small to be seen by the naked eye.

It was late spring in the southern hemisphere. The sun had barely risen, and we were once again starting our day very early because even under optimal conditions, finding, darting, and testing four lions for TB is a very tall order. Peter Rogers was the attending vet. There were also two other people on the team who specialized in the transfer of the animals to their new location once the tests had been performed. The process involved conducting the TB test while the lions were anesthetized. The lions would then be transferred to a quarantine facility, where they would be allowed to wake up. Three days later, they would once again be anesthetized, and the TB tests would be read.

We set off with the team in two game vehicles. Each vehicle had a game ranger armed and ready to use his weapon in defense of his charges. Peter and my team were in one of the vehicles, and the two game capture experts were in the other. It was thought that if we could initially locate just one or two of the lions, we may have success at locating the other two, and this would give us the possibility of actually doing all four lions in one day. As I said, this was a very tall order.

The African bush is a strange and wonderful place filled with the unexpected. When you set off to work in the bush, the panorama that unfolds is sometimes more breathtaking and astonishing than anything you could wish for. This was one of those days. Everyone wants to see a lion hunt and successfully kill its prey. Avid bush watchers occasionally see this. People who make game work their profession sit for days and weeks in order to be lucky enough to capture this event on film.

We were driving through dense bush following the tracks of a small pride of lions. The tracker Ocean was our guide once again. We had met him on our previous visit to Thornybush, when we were there to repair Mehlwane's eye. He remembered us and was pleased to see us. We were hot on the trail of this small pride, and according to Ocean, the pride included at least one of the lions scheduled to be moved. We were very close. Ocean was sitting in the tracker's seat and was directing us with hand signals. The animals were familiar with the vehicles and did not mind them, but they were often frightened by voices, so we kept quiet. Ocean gave the signal for the vehicle to stop, bent low, and pointed just ahead.

Suddenly, a young impala jumped out from the bush right in front of us, followed by a lioness. Then from an ambush position just in front of the impala, another lioness came out of the bush at full tilt and pounced upon the hapless impala, grabbing it by its neck. Usually a lion kills by clamping its powerful jaws around its prey's neck and suffocating the victim. This time, however, there were five hungry lions, and they literally ripped the small impala to shreds within the space of a minute or two. I have never seen an animal consumed so quickly in my entire experience in the bush. All that was left within a very short time were the two small horns and the hooves. There was a lot of growling and grunting, but the lions just kept at it until the impala was but a memory.

Within this group of lions were two of the lions we wanted to dart.

Peter had prepared a dart just in case we came across the correct lion and had a second dart at the ready. He loaded his gun with the dart and quietly took aim and shot one of the two lions. They were so busy chewing bones and resting after the feed that they hardly noticed the sound of the dart. The lion that was shot jumped up and growled but settled very quickly. Peter quietly loaded the second dart, and within a few seconds he had shot the second lion.

We now had two lions that would be sleeping within six minutes. Now was the time for the rangers and trackers to chase away the other lions. It is much safer to work on sleeping lions when the conscious ones are at a safe distance. We also didn't want to run the risk of one of the conscious lions attacking our two patients.

How, I asked myself, were the rangers going to chase away three large lions? I was only allowed to speculate on this for a short time. They climbed out of the car and clapped their hands and chased the lions away as though they were chasing a few small dogs. Unbelievably, the lions took fright and fled. A predator will even reluctantly give up its prey to someone who shouts and waves his hands with enough enthusiasm. (I've been told that this method, however, is not reliable when it comes to elephants, rhinos, and buffalo.) The tranquilizer had taken effect, and our two darted lions lay down in the bush and within six minutes were asleep.

We climbed out of the game vehicles now that it was safe and prepared for the TB test to be administered. We had already decided that the sleeping lions would be transferred to a quarantine facility nearby, and Peter radioed the other team to come help us load them into their vehicle. While they were on their way over to us, we got to work.

There is a lot of record keeping in TB testing. The lion's skin fold thickness is measured prior to the test being administered. This is done with a special set of calipers. The avian TB is then administered intradermally on the right side of the neck. An intradermal injection means that the injection deposits the fluid inside the skin of the lion, and not under it. After this is done, the bovine TB is injected on the left side of the neck. The measurements of the skin fold thickness of each side are recorded, along with the date and time of the test and the animal's name or number. This simple procedure was performed on both lions, and I acted as secretary by recording all the information in a dedicated notebook. By the time we had finished, the other game vehicle had arrived, and we loaded both lions into the back. An adult lion can weigh up to 300 kilograms (660 pounds), and it takes a team of strong men to lift a sleeping lion into the back of a truck. Once they had driven off, we were left to find the other two lions.

We had been lucky to find the first two so quickly. It was about two hours since we had started out, and we were ahead of schedule. We climbed back aboard the game vehicle and set off to find the tracks of the other lions. I have no idea how Ocean was able to distinguish between lions just by their tracks, but clearly he knew what he was doing. We drove back and forth across our path, cutting from side to side to pick up the other lions' tracks. After a half hour, we still had not found anything worth following. It was decided that the bush telegraph system would now be called in. It was getting warm by this time of the morning.

Thornybush is a working reserve, with many guests being driven around in as many as eight game vehicles at one time. Each vehicle has a tracker and a ranger, and they are equipped with radios. The head ranger, Mike Pieterse, was driving us around. We had worked with him as well when we repaired Mehlwane's eye. He radioed his colleagues, who were scattered all over the reserve, and told them what we were looking for. Once this was done, it was just a matter of time before one of the vehicles spotted our lions. While we waited, we drank coffee sweetened with condensed milk out in the middle of the bush. Life is filled with these special moments.

Suddenly, the radio crackled to life. One of our potential patients had been spotted, and we were given directions to his whereabouts. After about fifteen minutes of rough bush driving, we met up with the ranger who had spotted one of our quarries. He indicated to us where the lion was, then drove off with his load of guests. It was not really advisable for the paying guests to see what we were going to do, even though they groaned loudly at being left out of the action. Ocean was called in to examine the tracks, and he pronounced that it was in fact one of the lions we wanted. He sat in his tracking chair and directed us to where the lion lay. It was a solitary young male lion, about three-quarters grown. He was lying in the shade and looked as though he too had just fed.

Once again Peter was called in to administer the tranquilizing dart. Over the years of doing this, he had become quite good at guessing the weight of the animals that he treated. Our partially grown male was examined visually, and Peter determined the dose, taking into account his full belly as well. The dart was quietly fired into the recumbent lion's rump. The impact caused the lion to spring up in alarm and run off into the thick bush. We immediately followed the startled lion, and with Ocean's help, we were able to keep track of him until he went down. He appeared to be sleeping soundly, but this illusion was soon dispelled when we actually tried to move him. He raised his head and growled. He was very groggy, and his reactions were slow, but those teeth were still sharp, and the weight of his head driving those teeth into human flesh would be enough to do terrible damage. We had to administer another dose of anesthetic.

We performed the same procedure on him that we had done for the previous two lions. We now had a dilemma. We needed to find the fourth lion but could not leave this one lying asleep in the bush, even with a guard. The other vehicle was not due back from its trip to the quarantine station for another hour. We decided to load him into the back of Peter's vehicle and take him to the quarantine station ourselves. Despite our early start, time was suddenly not on our side. Administering the TB test had taken close to fifteen minutes. The loading took another fifteen minutes. The drive to the quarantine station and back was going to take at least an hour and a half. The other team had not yet returned from taking the two initial animals to the quarantine station, so the chances of finding the fourth lion that day seemed to be diminishing rapidly. We would have to make a judgment call soon as to whether or not we would be able to locate and test the fourth lion. We loaded number three and drove off with him. I sat in the back to tend to him while he slept.

The drug that we use to immobilize lions and keep them sleeping sometimes allows the animal to wake up but still be heavily sedated. This lion, which had already been given an extra dose, suddenly raised his head and looked at me. I nearly jumped out of my skin with fright. Fortunately, his head just flopped back down. There was not a lot of space in the back of the open truck, and we were traveling fairly fast. If I had needed help, it would have been difficult attracting Peter's attention. I had not had to call for Peter, so my dignity remained intact.

We eventually arrived at the quarantine station, and with the assistance of quite a few people working there, we transferred our sleeping patient to his temporary cage. Time had passed, and the sun was now a significant factor. We had three lions caged and tested. We would have about a two-hour window tonight to find number four.

Once this decision was made, we retired the team until that evening. Mike invited us back to the Thornybush lodge for one of their fantastic breakfasts. By the time we arrived, most of the guests had returned from their game drives, and several were curious about why we were there. Mike took the opportunity to educate them about the threat TB posed to African wildlife.

Peter left us to complete his rounds, and we made arrangements to meet up at four that afternoon. From mid-morning to late in the afternoon, the bush can be an inhospitable place. It can be hot and sometimes, just before the rains come, very humid as well. The clouds seem to magnify the sun's heat. All one could do during the heat of the day is lie around in the shade and pant and sweat. I empathized with and felt sorry for the animals in the bush. They too were find-ing whatever shade they could.

Four o'clock came slowly, and it was time to meet up again to find lion number four. If we could locate this last lion, we would really have done a day's work. We all climbed aboard one game vehicle, and Mike activated the bush tele-graph once again. He radioed the other vehicles that were just setting out for their afternoon drives and told them what we wanted. We drove around the area that this particular lion hunted in but could not find him. Despite the fact that we were working, we had the pleasure of seeing a female ele-phant and her very young calf, herds of buffalo, and many of the herbivores that populate the African plains. Don't for-get that even though these farms are privately owned and fenced, they still represent the vastness that is the southern African wilderness. The only difference between now and a few hundred years ago is that the wilderness areas have been parceled up and fenced. They are, however, expanding as more and more landowners turn their land over to private game reserves and stop cattle farming. Interestingly enough, the wild areas of southern Africa are growing.

Suddenly, our radio crackled to life. One of the other rangers had spotted what he thought was our last lion. It was about a twenty-minute drive from where we were. It was now after five, and even though it was summer, the sun was setting just after six o'clock. We were cutting it close, but we felt that it was worth the attempt. Mike drove as quickly as he could to the lion's location. Both Ocean and Mike confirmed that this was in fact the correct lion, and Peter quickly prepared his dart gun. This shot, however, was a difficult one because he had to aim through a thicket of trees. His aim was excellent, and the dart hit the lion in the shoulder. Luckily, we did not lose sight of him, because he only ran for about 100 meters (110 yards). He then lay down and within six minutes was asleep.

I had now helped in three TB tests, and this was my fourth. I was an old hand by now, and within five minutes of this lion falling asleep, we had administered the test. Next, we loaded the sleeping lion into the back of the truck, and then we set off for the quarantine station. The drive was forty-five minutes there. The sun was setting, and it really was getting quite dark by the time we set off. I sat once again in the back with the lion while we drove as fast as we safely could. This time there were no surprises, and the lion slept all the way without moving at all. When we arrived there, we once again assembled a team to carry our patient to a cage that would be his home for the next three days.

I stood back to survey the work that we had performed that day. There in front of me were four wild African lions in various stages of sedation and anesthesia. We had managed to capture them all and perform the TB tests we had set out to do, and they were all caged in the quarantine station waiting to have the results of the test read in three days' time. Only then would their fates be known. In the meantime, we had a tense wait.

The next day I drove to visit the caged lions at the quarantine station. I opened the enclosure where the cages were and walked slowly toward them. I knew that the drugs had worn off by now, but I was not prepared for what greeted me. I got to within 5 meters (16 feet) of the cages when suddenly all hell broke loose. All four lions charged the bars of their respective cages, and the gale of sound that assailed my ears was unbelievable. The volume of their roars from close quarters was enough to stun me almost senseless. I thanked my maker that the bars that stood between us were strong enough to withstand their charges. I hastily backed out of the enclosure. Peter in the meantime had come to see what all the commotion was about and had a little chuckle at my expense.

I stood a safe distance away and quietly observed the four lions pacing in their cages. The cages were in fact big enough to house each one for a few days. There were two compartments to each cage, and experienced handlers used hoses and water to encourage the lions to enter one compartment of the cage. Once this was done, a strong gate was dropped between the two parts to keep the lion in its compartment while the other compartment was cleaned. The lions were fed by placing meat in the clean section.

Sometimes three days can pass very quickly in the bush when one is game watching. This time, however, the time seemed to ooze slowly by because we had to wait three days to determine the results of the TB tests. We all wanted to immediately read the tests, but we had to wait the mandatory time to validate them. I've never felt so impatient in my life. Depending on the outcome of a test that I had played an intimate part in, the four lions would either go on to new homes to hunt and breed and do what all good lions do, or they would not be allowed to wake up from the anesthetic, but be destroyed and their carcasses burned.

The lions were each in their own cages and had been starved for twelve hours prior to the administration of the second round of anesthetics. They really roared and charged the bars as Peter approached them. He was used to this and did not flinch. Peter had a small dart gun that operated via compressed air, and using this, he surreptitiously administered the anesthetic dart to each of the gyrating lions. Once the drug kicked in, they started to get drowsy. They then all lay down in their cages and went to sleep. Once down, Peter and I climbed into their cages, and using the special calipers that are designed for TB testing, we measured the reactions on either side of their necks. It must have taken us about twenty minutes to finish reading the tests.

Relief washed over the entire crew as we announced that all four lions were TB free, and they could be certified as such. This enabled them to be moved to their new homes. The tension of the last three days melted away and was replaced by a quiet sense of relief and good feelings. There was no euthanasia to do, only relocation to their new home.

The two people who specialized in game transfer were part of the audience, and they had come prepared for the eventuality of a negative test. They had a large closed truck in which the four lions would easily fit. They also had transport crates to place each individual lion into. They sprang into action once they knew that the tests were negative. Each of the lions was individually crated, and then the crates were placed into the back of the truck. This took about an hour to do. Once packed, the lions were moved off and driven to their new homes about two hours away.

It is mandatory for all game animals to be tested prior to moving them from reserve to reserve. The consequences of taking a chance are horrendous. A reserve could be TB free prior to the introduction of a new animal. That new animal, however, may be the vector that brings TB to the reserve. It is beyond belief that there are still people in the game industry who have a very casual attitude toward TB. They try to get away with not testing for TB, or they try to tempt vets with bribes to "fudge" the tests. Luckily, most of the people working in my profession are honorable. Those that might engage in dishonest acts are few and far between. The profession takes TB very seriously, and with a lot of hard work and a bit of luck, this disease that is decimating the wildlife of Africa may one day be brought under control.

Acknowledgments

WHEN I WAS JUST A PUP, MY EARLIEST MEMORIES OF WHAT I WANTED TO do with my life revolved around becoming a veterinarian. I did not want to be a firefighter or a doctor or even a train engineer. I have been fortunate to realize my dream, and I have enjoyed every minute of it. If my own children were to ask me for advice on which career to choose, I would tell them to become vets too.

After all my trekking through South Africa, I always return to my practice in Cape Town, the source of my joy, my income, and many of my adventures. I have a saying: If every day I learn something new while plying my profession, then one day when I die, I may be just less than a fool. Every day of my professional life I get the chance to sit on the floor and play with animals, petting them while I examine them. What amazes me is that I actually get paid to do this.

My career choice has afforded me the opportunity to meet and interact with amazing people and amazing animals. I have been given the opportunity to travel extensively throughout South Africa to view the vast tracts of land dedicated to the conservation of Africa's game animals. I live in Bantry Bay, a coastal suburb on the Atlantic seaboard of Cape Town, where I can stand on my patio that overlooks the ocean and see whales breaching in the sea a few hundred yards away. The water sometimes roils with dolphins and seals. If

I look the other way, I am overwhelmed by the view of Table Mountain, a world famous landmark, as well as Lion's Head and Signal Hill. I am surrounded by nature even in the heart of the city. South Africa is blessed with natural abundance, and I am blessed to be a part of it.

When we think of African wildlife, we usually think of the "Big Five" and animals of the African plains. To see these animals today, though, you need to travel outside the city and a bit farther afield. There are areas closer to where I live, within a few hours' drive, where private reserves have sprung up. People have purchased farms and have reintroduced game animals onto the land, thereby creating eco-friendly, tourist-oriented reserves. While these ventures may be convenient, they do not give what I have come to view as a truly African experience. Kruger National Park in the northeast corner of South Africa, however, epitomizes what I consider to be great game reserve territory. Kruger has numerous smaller private reserves tacked onto its western border, and by mutual agreement, the fences that once separated the reserves from the park have been removed, thus affording wild animals more access to traditional migratory routes.

To the east of Kruger lie the Lebombo Mountains, which form a natural border between South Africa and Mozambique. These mountains and the surrounding area in Mozambique also have large tracts of land dedicated to game. By agreement among South Africa and its neighbors, Zambia and Mozambique, the game and border fences are being removed, and the animals that now call this area home can once more follow the routes of their ancestors that were accessible prior to man coming in and carving the land up into smaller and smaller parcels.

The removal of these border fences has ensured that the land mass dedicated to wildlife has not only been enlarged but also that the traditional migratory routes that animals have followed for eons have been restored. For this, the various wildlife authorities must be congratulated, complimented, and thanked profusely.

The tales I have collected here reflect just some of the people I have met along the way who have inspired me. One of the most influential people who shaped my career as a vet is Professor Jan Le Roux. He was a professor of anatomy at the University of Pretoria and the very first lecturer I encountered in my studies. His amazing way with words and encyclopedic knowledge of anatomy made an indelible impression on me. For instance, when we were studying equine anatomy, he would often say, "No hoof, no horse." This reminder to first attend to the basics before getting involved in the details has served me well throughout my career. Professor Le Roux also liked to say, "The similarities between species are vast; the differences are few and far between." These words came back to me every time I worked on a different animal, from Monty, the squirrel monkey, to Jabu, the elephant. Professor Le Roux's message again was to go back to basics and look for the common thread. That's usually what solves the problem.

Dr. Dave Meltzer was another lecturer at the University of Pretoria while I was there. He went on to chair the wildlife department and became one of the foremost authorities on cheetah reproduction. He has, sadly, passed on, but he left an amazing legacy. Almost single-handedly, he helped to ensure the survival of the species.

I spent five and a half years at the University of Pretoria and was overwhelmingly happy there. I am thrilled to say that even today this amazing school produces results that astonish the world. All of us who went there were privileged to have done so, and the education we received was superb.

Another person I must mention here is Dr. Fritz Huchzermeyer, now an elder statesman of our profession. He spent five years on the Galapagos Islands studying tortoises, reptiles, and strange mammals. He is also an expert in crocodiles and ostriches. If I ever have questions about tortoises and other species he knows well, he is always generous in sharing his knowledge.

I have enjoyed many adventures with Dr. Huchzermeyer's son, David, who is also a veterinarian with a master's degree in fish. David's son is now studying at the University of Cape Town a few miles from my home, so every once in a while we meet and barbecue together.

George Mazarakis, the executive producer of South Africa's investigative TV show Carte Blanche, was the first person who saw merit in my ideas. I owe a debt of gratitude to him for the faith he showed in me. We worked together for three years, and even after parting ways professionally, we have maintained a strong friendship. When he occasionally visits Cape Town, I am one of the people he contacts despite his very busy agenda.

The many game rangers I have met and worked with over the years are the "grease" that makes the game reserve engine run. Without them, there would be no game reserve industry. My thanks go to the many I have met, especially Ross Dunbar from Tshukudu and Mike Pieterse from Thornybush. I am thankful for the hospitality I have enjoyed at some of the great private game reserves, and it has been a privilege to savor Africa in all its splendor.

My friend and colleague Dr. Peter Rogers has a special place in my heart. Peter and I started our veterinary studies together and have been friends ever since. We have shared many special adventures and good times. Peter has chosen a career as a wildlife veterinarian and has based himself in Hoedspruit, a small bushveld town nestled in the foothills of the Drakensberg Mountains in the South African lowveld. He has a successful wildlife practice in Hoedspruit, and every day of his life is an action movie. He will anesthetize an elephant, a rhino, a lion, and a leopard, all on the same day, then go back to his hospital and spay a dog or a cat. His meticulous attention to detail has saved many an animal. Most of my wildlife adventures have been in Peter's company, and if it were not for him and the friendship we enjoy, my life would be immeasurably poorer.

I must also thank Braam Malherbe, who has enriched my practice by bringing many exotic animals to my office for help. Braam, incidentally, and his partner were the first to run the Great Wall of China in one expedition, a world first. They ran twenty-five miles a day for four months.

Finally, my wife, Kathy, and daughters, Alexis, Samantha, and Jamie, deserve special mention. They have given me immense joy, and through them I truly have discovered the meaning of life. I am deeply indebted and forever grateful to Kathy, who took over and ran our private practice while I was off gallivanting in bush country. Kathy, I owe you big and promise you lots of bush holidays soon.

I dedicate *Tales of an African Vet* to Kathy, Lexi, Sam, and Jamie. Because of your support, love, and astonishing patience, I have been able to pursue my dream to its fullest, and we as a family can be proud of this book. I wrote the words, but you all made the dream come true.

Index

About the Author

Dr. Roy Aronson graduated as a vet in 1984 from the University of Pretoria school of veterinary medicine. He works mainly with dogs and cats and some exotic pets that come his way but has also had the opportunity to work extensively with African wildlife. In his spare time he likes to exercise at the gym, paddle on the ocean, and hike in the mountains.

He lives in Cape Town with his wife, Kathy, also a qualified vet who has a great passion for horses. They have three children, Alexis, Samantha, and Jamie.

4/11